Dr. Glenn Orr

Are the Mormons Teaching Fables

"And they shall turn away their ears from the truth,
and shall be turned unto fables"
2 Timothy 4:3-4

outskirts press

Are the Mormons Teaching Fables
"And they shall turn away their ears from the truth, and shall be turned unto fables"
All Rights Reserved.
Copyright © 2023 Dr. Glenn Orr
v4.0

The opinions expressed in this manuscript are solely the opinions of the author and do not represent the opinions or thoughts of the publisher. The author has represented and warranted full ownership and/or legal right to publish all the materials in this book.

This book may not be reproduced, transmitted, or stored in whole or in part by any means, including graphic, electronic, or mechanical without the express written consent of the publisher except in the case of brief quotations embodied in critical articles and reviews.

Outskirts Press, Inc.
http://www.outskirtspress.com

Paperback ISBN: 978-1-9772-6149-6
Hardback ISBN: 978-1-9772-6186-1

Library of Congress Control Number: 2023903811

Cover Photo © 2023 www.gettyimages.com. All rights reserved - used with permission.

Outskirts Press and the "OP" logo are trademarks belonging to Outskirts Press, Inc.

PRINTED IN THE UNITED STATES OF AMERICA

Table of Contents

Chapter 1: Where Did Paul Get His Doctrine? 1

Chapter 2: What Was Paul's Doctrine? ....1...3

Chapter 3: Let's Talk About the Book of Mormon..............27

Chapter 4: What Then Is the Purpose of the Book of Mormon? 33

Chapter 5: Archaeological Evidences 35

Chapter 6: Truthfulness of the Witnesses............................43

Chapter 7: Do We Need to Pray About It? 51

Chapter 8: How Did a French Word Get in the Book of Mormon? Jacob 7:27 57

Chapter 9: Is the Book of Mormon True? 59

Chapter 10: A Catholic Priest Comments on the Book of Mormon 61

Chapter 11: You Mormons Are All Ignoramuses! 63

Chapter 12: Exodus from Jerusalem 67

Chapter 13: Could Anyone in the United States Have Known of It in 1829?..71

Chapter 14: Chiasmus 73

Chapter 15: Wordprint..75

Chapter 16: The Anti's Claim It Was Written in the Nineteenth Century.............................79

Chapter 17: Can You Duplicate It?..85

Chapter 18: The Power of Prophecy 93

Chapter 19: Prophecies of Joseph Smith, Jr........................107

Chapter 20: Tests to Show Mormons Are a Cult................117

Chapter 21: Why Do You Say on the Cover, "Skeptical and Scriptural" in Your Review? ...119

Chapter 22: Contradictions in the New Testament..............123

Chapter 23: Questions Regarding the Church of Jesus Christ of Latter Day Saints.....................141

The Book

ARE THE MORMONS TEACHING FABLES?

Paul, in 2 Timothy 4:3 says, "For the time will come when they will not endure sound doctrine; but after their own lusts shall they heap to themselves teachers, having itching ears," (ie., entertaining them – telling them what they want to hear). Verse 4 continues, "And they shall turn away their ears from the truth, and shall be turned unto fables.

Merium-Webster defines Fables as a fictitious practice or statement, a falsehood

ARE THE MORMONS TEACHING FAISEHOODS? HOW DO WE KNOW?

Paul also in Galatians 1:8 says, "But though we, or an angel from heaven, preach any other gospel unto you than that which we have preached unto you, let him be accursed."Verse

9 repeats,"As we said before, So say I now again, if any man preach any other gospel unto you than that ye have received, from me, (Paul, he means if you read it in context) let him be accursed."

ARE THE MORMONS THE ACCURSED?? HOW DO WE FIND OUT? PAUL HAS GIVEN US THE ANSWER. THE ONES THAT TEACH A DIFFERENT GOSPEL THAN THAT WHICH PAUL TEACHES ARE THE ACCURSED.

CHAPTER 1

Where Did Paul Get His Doctrine?

In Galatians 1:12 Paul says,"But I certify you, brethren, that the gospel which was preached of (by) me is not after {from a} man. For I neither received it (of man), neither was I taught it, (by man) but by the revelation of Jesus Christ." According to Paul he was taught for three years before he visited the other Apostles.

CHAPTER 2

What Was Paul's Doctrine?

SINCE PAUL RECEIVED THE GOSPEL DIRECTLY FROM JESUS CHRIST, IF ANY GOSPEL IS PURE, IT WOULD BE PAUL'S, RIGHT? I.E., IT WOULD BE THE NEW TESTAMENT GOSPEL. THEN LET'S EXAMINE WHAT PAUL TAUGHT:

1. **GOD THE FATHER AND JESUS CHRIST ARE SEPARATE PERSONAGES, NOT JUST OF SPIRIT OR ESSENCE OR MIST**

    1. First of all, Paul was present when Stephen was being stoned to death and he saw Stephen transfigured before him when Stephen saw God the Father and Jesus Christ as separate personages. Acts 7:55-60.

2. Hebrews 1:1-3 "God, who at sundry times and in divers manners... Hath in these last days spoken to us by his Son...Who being the brightness of his glory, <u>and the express image of his (God's) person</u>... Sat down on the right hand of the Majesty on high; (God)" If Jesus was created in the express image of God, how can anyone believe God is an "essence"? Essence is defined by Merriiam Webster as a spirit or immaterial entity. Some then would interpret God as a cloud or a mist! It is reported that all Protestant churches believe the "essence" theory which originated with the Catholic Church and has been the doctrine since 325 A D when the Nicene Creed was agreed upon by approximately 318 Bishops of the Catholic Church. In writing about the Creed, Eusebius Habilis, Bishop of Caesarea, one of the main Bishops in the formation of the Nicene Creed, wrote to his people a letter in which he said, ..." and that the Son (Jesus Christ) did not subsist from the Father (God) either by division or abscission (being cut off a piece from-here is that essence or cloud or mist theory- since it was impossible that an immaterial, intellectual and incorporeal (without body) nature could admit of any bodily affection." This latter part is a description of God, according to most churches today. I.e., God is a mist or essence, not a personage with a body, as Paul states. By the way, how could Paul know that God and Jesus look exactly

alike? Because he was caught up in the third heaven and saw God and Jesus! 2 Corinthians 12:2

3. Romans 8:34 Paul says, "Christ. . who is even at the right hand of God." . How can you be at the right hand of God unless God is a person with a body with hands, etc.?

4. Paul says in 2 Corinthians 4:4 "In whom the god of this world (Satan) had blinded the minds of them which believe not, lest the light of the glorious gospel of Christ, who is <u>the image of God</u>, should shine unto them."

5. James also taught the same doctrine in James 3:9 when he said that we are "... made after the similitude of God. "This simply ratifies the statement made in Genesis 1:26 where it says, "And God said, let us make man in our image, after our likeness" if God is an essence or a vapor, mist or cloud, are we then little mists??

6. John taught the same in 1 John 3:

WHAT DO THE MORMONS TEACH?

1. The above Scriptures plus the following:

2. Mosiah 7:27 King Lemhi says, "... or in other words, he (the prophet) said that man was created after the image of God."

3. D&C 20:18 Jesus said, "...and that he (God) created man, male and female, after his own image and in his own likeness, created He them."

4. D&C 130:22 Joseph Smith had it revealed to him, "The Father has a body of flesh and bones as tangible as man's; the Son also; but the Holy Ghost has not a body of flesh and bones, but is a personage of Spirit. Were it not so, the Holy Ghost could not dwell in us." This is what the Catholic (universal) church did not understand in 325 A.D. when it developed the Nicene Creed and is the basis for the confusion today. **They have confused God with the Holy Ghost!**

2. JESUS CHRIST CREATED THIS WORLD AND OTHER WORLDS

1. Hebrews 1:1-2 Paul says, "God hath in these last days spoken to us by his Son, whom he appointed heir of all things, by whom he also made the worlds."

2. Ephesians 3:9 Paul says, "God, who created all things by Jesus Christ."

3. There are more but these should suffice.

WHAT DO THE MORMONS TEACH?

1. The above Scriptures **PLUS THE FOLLOWING:**

2. D&C 38:3 Jesus Christ and the same which spake, and the world was made.

3. D&C 76:24 by him (Jesus Christ) the worlds are and were created (Note the s on worlds)

3. THERE WAS A LIFE BEFORE THIS LIFE

1. Romans 8:29 Paul, talking about the creation of man says, "For whom he (God) did foreknow, he also did predestinate to be conformed to the image of his Son." In other words, God knew us before we were born into this life.

2. Ephesians 1:4-5 Paul says, "According as he (God) has chosen us in him before the foundation of the world that we should be holy and without blame before him in love: having predestined us" In other words, we were with God before this world was even formed. He knew us..

3. II Timothy 1:9 Paul says, "God; who hath saved us, and called us with a holy calling, not according to our works, but according to his own purpose and grace, which was given us in Christ Jesus <u>before the world began.</u>"

WHAT DO THE MORMONS TEACH?

1. The above scriptures plus the following:

2. Alma 13:3 High Priests were called and "...prepared from the foundation of the world according to the foreknowledge of God, on account of their exceeding faith and good works; among them was Melchizedek

3. Moses 3:5 "For I, the Lord God, Created all things, of which I have spoken, spiritually, before they were

naturally upon the face of the earth ,,, for in heaven created I them; and there was not yet flesh upon the earth, neither in the water, neither in the air;" ; This probably explains our preexistence better than any other place.

4. JESUS ATONED FOR OUR SINS BUT WE MUST DO MORE THAN SIMPLY BELIEVE BECAUSE WE WILL BE JUDGED BY OUR WORKS AT RESURRECTION. SIMPLY SAYING, I BELIEVE, AND DOING YOUR OWN THING WON'T PLACE US IN THE PRESENCE OF GOD IN THE LIFE AFTER THIS LIFE.

1. Romans 3:23-25 Paul says, "For all have sinned, and come short of the glory of God; being justified (cleansed) freely by his grace through the redemption that is in Christ Jesus: whom God has sent forth to be a propitiation through faith in his blood." Propitiation means to cleanse.

2. Romans 5:11 Paul actually spends the whole chapter talking about the free gift to us of the atonement of Jesus Christ and how important it is to us to show that we can be forgiven of our sins, that we no longer need to be stoned to death for adultery, for example.

3. Ephesians 2:1 Paul says, And you hath he quickened (made alive) who were dead in trespasses and sins. For by grace (gift) are ye saved (from trespasses and sins) through faith; and not of yourselves:; it is the gift of God: (through the atonement of Jesus Christ): 9 Not of

works, (This was in rebuttal to the Judaizers) lest any man should boast." Probably one of the most misinterpreted verses in the Bible. They don't read it in context, instead just interpret it to mean that all they have to do is believe to be saved in the kingdom of God, no matter how many sins they commit. If they are correct, why did Paul spend the entire chapter 6 telling people to be good? Or why, in the preceding book, Galatians 6:4-5, did Paul say, "But let let every man prove his own work, and then shall he have rejoicing in himself alone, and not in another, For every man shall bear his own burden. And in seven. Be not deceived; God is not mocked; for whatsoever a man soweth, that shall he also reap. Okay how about instant forgiveness through the atonement by merely confessing and doing the sin again and confessing again etc., etc.? Such do not understand the process of repentance. Or else they forget to read Hebrews 10:26 in which Paul says, " For if we sin willfully after that we have received the knowledge of the truth, there remains no more sacrifice (atonement) for sins."

WHAT DO THE MORMONS TEACH?

1. The above Scriptures **PLUS THE FOLLOWING:**
2. The Atonement and the importance of it is mentioned 17 times in the book of Mormon and 10 times in the Doctrine and Covenants.

3. In the Articles of Faith Number 3: It states, We believe that through the Atonement of Christ, all mankind may be saved by obedience to the laws and ordinances of the gospel.

4. Alma 5:31 "he must repent or he cannot be saved."

5. Alma 34:33 "do not procrastinate the day of your repentance."

6. There are about 50 places in the Book of Mormon where it talks about the necessity of repentance.

7. In the Articles of Faith #4, it states, "We believe that the first principles of the gospel are: first, faith in the Lord Jesus Christ, second repentance, third baptism by immersion for the remission of sins and fourth laying on of hands for the gift of the Holy Ghost."

8. D&C 82:3 "For of him unto whom much is given much is required; and he who sins against the greater light shall receive the greater condemnation."

9. D&C 82:7 "but unto that soul who sinneth (after having repented of the same sin) shall the former sins return. saith the Lord your God."

5. BAPTISM IS BY IMMERSION

1. in Acts 8:38, Luke tells us of Philip baptizing the eunuch: "And he (the eunuch) commanded the chariot to stand still: and they went down both into the water, both

Philip and the eunuch; and he (Philip) baptized him. . You don't go down into the water to sprinkle, you bury them in the water as Paul taught.

2. In Colossians 2:12 Paul teaches, "Buried with him (Jesus Chris) in baptism wherein also ye are risen with him through the faith of the operation of God, who hath raised him (Jesus Christ) from the dead."

3. In Romans 6:4 Paul teaches, "Therefore we are buried with him by baptism into death: that like as Christ was raised up from the dead by the glory of the Father, even so we also should walk in newness of life."

WHAT DO THE MORMONS TEACH?

1. The above scriptures **PLUS THE FOLLOWING:**
2. Mosiah 18:14 …"were buried in the water".
3. 3 Nephi 11:26 …"immerse them in the water."
4. 3 Nephi 19:13 (following baptism) …" had come up out of the water."
5. D&C 20:74 …"immerse him or her in the water."
6. See Articles of Faith #4

6. PROPER ORGANIZATION OF THE CHURCH

1. Paul teaches in Ephesians 4:11-12, "And he (Jesus Christ) gave some, apostles; and some, prophets; and some, evangelists; and some, pastors and teachers; For

the perfecting of the saints, (followers of Jesus Christ." That is why we are called the Church of Jesus Christ of Latter-Day Saints, to distinguish us from the early day saints or what is called the Primitive Church. ..." for the work of the ministry, for the edifying of the body (Church) of Christ." Paul went on in verse 14 to tell the purpose of these offices, …"that we henceforth be no more children, tossed to and fro, and carried about with every wind of doctrine, by the sleight of men, and cunning craftiness, whereby they lie in wait to deceive."

2. Paul teaches in I Corinthians 12:28 the same thing, "And God has set some in the church, first apostles, secondarily prophets, thirdly teachers…"

3. In Ephesians 2:20 Paul says of the saints at Ephesus that they are of the …"household (church) of God and are built upon the foundation of the apostles and prophets, Jesus Christ himself being the chief cornerstone."

WHAT DO THE MORMONS TEACH?

1. The above Scriptures **PLUS THE FOLLOWING:**

2. Articles of Faith #6: "We believe in the same organization that existed in the Primitive Church, namely, apostles, prophets, pastors, teachers, evangelists and so forth."

7. PAUL TAUGHT THE GIFTS OF TONGUES, REVELATION, HEALINGS, PROPHECY, ETC.

1. Paul teaches in 1 Corinthians Chapter 12 about the different gifts and in chapter 14 he spends almost the whole chapter talking about the gift of tongues and the interpretation thereof.

2. Paul taught in first Corinthians chapter 4:7 "For who maketh thee to differ from another? (Who gives you the gifts to start with?) and what hast thou that thou didst not receive?(from God) now if thou didst receive it, (from God) why dost thou glory (brag), as if thou hadst not received it (from God)?" In other words, if we have talents or gifts such as the gift of languages, mathematics, history or athleticisim, we shouldn't brag about them, we should be humble as the gift came from God, not of our doing.

WHAT DO THE MORMONS TEACH?

1. The above Scriptures **PLUS THE FOLLOWING:**:

2. Alma 9:21 in talking about the offspring of Lehigh, talks about all the help from the Lord they have received, including revelation, prophecy, being fed in the wilderness, gifts of tongues, healing, preaching and the gift of the Holy Ghost and the gift of translation.

3. Many others. Also the Articles of Faith #7: We believe in the gift of tongues, prophecy, revelation, visions, healing, interpretation of tongues, and so forth.

8. PAUL TAUGHT NOT ONLY BY WORD BUT BY EXAMPLE THAT THERE SHOULD BE AN UNPAID MINISTRY.

1. Paul taught in 2 Thessalonians 3: 8-10, "Neither did we (he and his fellow ministers) eat any man's bread for naught; but wrought with labor and travail night and day, that we might not be chargeable to any of you."

2. Acts 20:33-35 Paul is talking to the brethren at Ephesus and telling them that he has labored among them for three years, "night and day with tears." Then he says, "I have coveted no man's silver, or gold, or apparel, yea, ye yourselves know, that these hands have ministered unto my necessities, and to them that were with me. I have shewed you all things, how that so laboring ye ought to support the weak, and you remember the words of the Lord Jesus, how he said it is more blessed to give than receive." So Paul provided not only for his own welfare but the disciples that were with him. In addition he helps support the weak and he exhorts the brethren to do the same.

3. 1 Corinthians 9:11 Paul tells the people of Corinth (in Greece of today) "if we have sown unto you spiritual

What Was Paul's Doctrine?

things, is it a great thing if we shall reap your carnal things?" By that he is saying that he has the power to receive money for preaching. Then in verse 13 he tells them that the priests in the temple live off the things of the temple. But then in verse 15 Paul says, "But I have used none of these things: neither have I written these things, (temple offerings or temple meat from the sacrifices) that it should be so done unto me: <u>for it were better for me to die, then any man should make my glorying void.</u>" So here he is explaining why he does not accept money or meat to–it would make his glory void. In other words if he accepted payment it would take away the glory that he hopes for in the next life. **WE CAN'T BE PAID TWICE!!**

4. In Paul's letter to Titus, he says, starting in verse 10 of chapter 1: "For there are many unruly and vain talkers and deceivers, specially they of the circumcision; (Jews) 11. Whose mouths must be stopped, who subvert whole houses, teaching things which they ought not, <u>for filthy lucre's sake.</u>" Peter preaches exactly the same thing in 1 Peter 5 2-4. In verse 2 Peter, in talking to the Elders, says, "Feed (spiritually) the flock (Church) of God... not for filthy lucre.." In verse 4 Peter explains why when he says, "And when the chief Shepherd (Jesus Christ) shall appear (at resurrection), <u>ye shall receive a crown of glory that fadeth not away.</u>" Now, back to Paul. Paul becomes more specific in his direction in

1 Corinthians 9:18. "What is my reward then? Verily that, when I preach the gospel, I may make the gospel of Christ without charge, that I abuse not my power in the gospel." He did this so that he could be free from all men. If they gave him money they might influence his ministry.

WHAT DO THE MORMONS TEACH?

1. The above Scriptures **PLUS THE FOLLOWING:**
2. 2 Nephi 2:4 Lehigh is conferring his last blessing on his children and he tells Jacob that "salvation is free." We do not have to buy, nor can we, our resurrection nor our forgiveness of sin. Jesus paid dearly for us. The same thing is said in 2 Nephi 26:27 "but he had given it (salvation) free for all men;"
3. 2 Nephi 26:29 Nephi talks of his time which turns out to be prophecy of our time as well: "He (Lord God) commanded that there shall be no priestcrafts; for, behold, priestcrafts are that men preach and set themselves up for a light unto the world, that they may get gain and praise of the world; but they seek not the welfare of Zion."
4. In 2 Nephi 26:31, Nephi nails them: "But the laborer (minister) and Zion shall labor for Zion; <u>for if they labor for money they shall perish.</u>"
5. In Matthew 10:9 Jesus says, in talking to the Twelve, "... Freely ye have received, freely give."

9. PAUL TAUGHT THE THREE DEGREES OF GLORY IN HEAVEN, ALTHOUGH THE TRANSLATORS HAVE LEFT OUT PART.

1. In 1 Corinthians, Chapter 15, Paul is talking to the people of Corinth who had stopped believing in resurrection. In verse 40 the translators have only left two degrees in but the third-telestial-has been left out. However, in verse 41, talking about the degrees of heaven or glory, the translators left in the three, as to the difference in the glory (or brightness) of the three.

2. Obviously, Paul knew of the three degrees of glory, as he says in 2 Corinthians 12: 2, "I knew a man (himself) caught up in the third heaven." This would mean the Celestial Kingdom, where God and Christ dwell.

WHAT DO THE MORMONS TEACH?

1. The above **PLUS THE FOLLOWING:**
2. A great deal of clarification exists in the Doctrine and Covenants. In the preface to D&C 76 Joseph Smith says on February 6, 1832, "Upon the return from the Amherst Conference, I resumed the translation of the Scriptures (In this case, referring to the New Testament) From sundry (many) revelations which had been received, it was apparent that many important points touching the salvation of man had been taken from the Bible, or lost

before it was compiled. It appeared self-evident (from the information in the New Testament) from the truths that were left, that if God rewarded every one according to the deeds done in the body, the term Heaven as intended for the Saints' (followers of Jesus Christ) eternal home, must include more kingdoms than one." As a result he received the following vision: D&C 76:70 After describing who will be there it says, "these are they whose bodies are celestial, whose glory is that of the sun, even the glory is that of the sun, even the glory of God, the highest of all". Next is the terrestrial glory of Heaven. 77-78 "These are they who receive of the presence of the Son, but not of the fullness of the Father. Wherefore, they are bodies terrestrial, and not bodies celestial, and differ in glory as the moon differs from the sun. These are they who are not valiant in the testimony of Jesus…" D&C 76:81 "And again, we saw the glory of the telestial, which glory is that of the lesser, even as the glory of the stars differs from that of the glory of the moon in the firmament."

3. In D&C 88:22-23 elaborates further: "For he who is not able to abide the law of the celestial kingdom cannot abide a celestial glory. (As bright as the sun) And he who cannot abide the law of the terrestrial kingdom cannot abide a terrestrial glory." (comparing it to the brightness of the moon) To define "glory" we can look to verse 28 where it talks about that glory or light: "and

your glory shall be that glory by which your bodies are quickened." (Made alive)

10. BY EXAMPLE, PAUL TAUGHT YOU MUST HAVE THE AUTHORITY TO BAPTIZE AND TO GIVE THE GIFT OF THE HOLY GHOST.

1. In Acts 19:1-4, Paul is in Ephesus and meets some disciples and asks them if they have received the Holy Ghost and they didn't know what it was. They had been baptized unto John. So, in verse 5, Luke says, "When they heard this, they were baptized in the name of the Lord Jesus. 6. And when Paul had laid his hands upon them, the Holy Ghost came on them; and they spake with tongues, and prophesied." So it was necessary for Paul to rebaptize them and then give them the gift of the Holy Ghost by the laying on of hands because he had the authority.

WHAT DO THE MORMONS TEACH?

1. The above **PLUS THE FOLLOWING:**

2. In Mosiah 21:33 King Lemhi was aware we can't just assume the authority: "And it came to pass that King Lemhi and many of his people were desirous to be baptized; but there was none in the land that had authority from God."

3. D&C 42:11 Again I say unto you, that it shall not be given to anyone to go forth to preach my gospel, or to build up my church, except he be ordained by someone who has authority… and he has been regularly ordained."

4. D&C 107:20 "The power and authority of the lesser, or Aaronic Priesthood, is to administer in outward ordinances, the letter of the gospel, the baptism of repentance for the remission of sins"

5. D&C 20:38 "The duty of the elders, 41 and to confirm those who are baptized into the church, by the laying on of hands for the baptism of fire and the Holy Ghost, according to the Scriptures."

6. The authority to baptize was restored to the earth by John the Baptist, May 15, 1829, on the banks of the Susquehanna River, between Harmony and Colesville, Pennsylvania to Joseph Smith and Oliver Cowdery, while they were yet translating the plates which translation became known as the Book of Mormon, Another Testament of Jesus Christ. In the month of June, 1829, they received the power to confer the gift of the Holy Ghost, that great Comforter and Teacher of Truth by which we can know the truth of all things.

7. The authority has been handed down from time to time to the present. I can trace my authority to baptize back in 10 ordinations to Jesus Christ! What a beautiful feeling to know that the authority has been restored and

I have not just taken it upon myself nor "assumed" I have the authority. That would be like assuming I have the authority to be a policeman when all I did was put on the uniform. You should want to see my badge and check my authenticity.

11. IT IS NECESSARY TO TAKE CARE OF THE POOR.

1. Paul says it is necessary to take care of the poor. He did it by example in Acts 20:33-35. Also in Galatians 2:10 it talks about the necessity of taking care of the poor.

WHAT DO THE MORMONS TEACH?

1. The above **PLUS THE FOLLOWING:**
2. The Mormons probably do by far the best job in the world of "taking care of their own". In the welfare program of the United States, made necessary by the default of man to take care of the poor, less than 5% of the money spent ends up in the hands of the recipient. The rest goes for the administration of the program. In the Church Welfare Program, 95% of the funds end up in the hands of the recipient. A friend of mine, Les Wilson, was (now retired) a manager of the Oklahoma City Social Security office. Years ago, when I heard those statistics I asked him if they were true regarding the U S Social Security statistics. He said, "They are probably more lopsided than that!"

3. D&C 83:6 "And the storehouse shall be kept by the consecrations (donations) of the church; and widows and orphans shall be provided for, as also the poor."

4. There are probably 30 scriptures in the Book of Mormon and the Doctrine and Covenants which command us to take care of the poor and the needy.

5. In our tornado of May 20, 2013 the two most numerous groups, according to one of the television stations were "The Mormons and the second was the Church of Jesus Christ of Latter Day Saints." The same people!

12. WE SHOULD BE OPEN MINDED FOR ADDITIONAL TRUTHS INCLUDING SCRIPTURES. PAUL SAYS IN PHILIPPIANS 4:8, "Finally, brethren, whatsoever things are true, whatsoever things are honest, whatsoever things are just, whatsoever things are pure, whatsoever things are lovely, whatsoever things are of good report; if there be any virtue, and if there be any praise, think on these things."

1. Many people misinterpret John in the Book of Revelations when he says in 22:18-19, "For I testify unto every man that heareth the words of the prophecy of this book, if any man shall add unto these things, God shall add unto him the plagues that are written in this book:" 19 goes on and states that no man is to take away from the prophecies either. Therefore, some use this to

mean that we should not add to nor take away from the Bible. I will try to correct this.

2. John was referring to the Book of Revelations, not to the whole Bible. By the time John wrote the Book of Revelations, there had already been some tinkering with some of the other writings that are now found in the New Testament. The word Bible is taken from the Greek word, "ta biblia" which means the books. (note the plural).

3. The Book of Revelations was not the last book or letter to be written, even by John! 1, 2, 3 John, according to Bible scholars, were written some 6 to 7 years after the Book of Revelations.

4. Just getting it to English (much less Aramic, Hebrew and Latin) the Bible went through a whole series of "add tos" and "takeaways" in the numerous translations over the centuries, getting to the King James version, adding and taking away old books. Since its compilation in 1611 there have been numerous other translations that have gone through the same process.

5. If we took John literally, we should not consider his book or any books past Deuteronomy because Moses states virtually the same thing in Deuteronomy 4:2 when he says, "ye shall not add unto the word which I command you, neither shall ye diminish ought from it, that ye may keep the commandments of the Lord your God which I command you."

6. We realize no Bible scholar would ever use Revelations 22:18-19 to refute Paul's statement because of all the evidence stated above.

WHAT DO THE MORMONS TEACH?

1. The above **PLUS THE FOLLOWING:**

2. We are extremely fortunate to have additional scriptures such as the Book of Mormon, An Additional Testament That Jesus Is the Christ, Translated by the gift and power of God, through a 25-year-old man with a third grade formal education at the time it was published. By the way, this level of formal education was not unusual on the frontier in the farming communities in the early 1800s.

3. D&C 20:35 says, "And when we know that these things (Forgiveness, repentance, baptism, enduring to the end, etc.,) are true and according to the revelations of John, neither adding to, nor diminishing from the prophecy of his book, the holy Scriptures, or the revelations of God which shall come hereafter by the gift and power of the Holy Ghost, the voice of God, or ministering angels." In other words, we neither add to nor take away from John's revelations.

4. Articles of Faith 9: "We believe all that God has revealed, all that he does now reveal, and we believe that He will yet reveal many great and important things pertaining to the Kingdom of God."

5. Articles of Faith Thirteen: "We believe in being honest, true, chaste, benevolent, virtuous and in doing good to all men; indeed, we may say that we follow the admonition of Paul-We believe all things, we hope all things, we have endured many things and we hope to endure all things.If there is anything virtuous, lovely, or of good report or praiseworthy, we seek after these things.

CONCLUSION: IF WE ARE A NEW TESTAMENT CHURCH AS DEFINED BY PAUL, AN EARLY DAY APOSTLE OF JESUS CHRIST, WE MUST TEACH THE FOLLOWING OR WE ARE TEACHING FABLES:

1. **God and Jesus Christ are separate corporeal personages**
2. **Jesus Christ created this world and other worlds**
3. **There is a life before this life**
4. **We will be judged by our works**
5. **We must be baptized by immersion by one who has the authority**
6. **There must be the proper organization of the Church.**
7. **We must believe in the gifts of tongues, revelation, healings, prophecy, etc.**
8. **We must have a unpaid ministry**
9. **We must teach that there are 3 degrees of Heaven**

10. It is necessary to take care of the poor

11. We must be open-minded and not limit God in additional revelations

You can see that the only church that practices all of what Paul taught is the Church of Jesus Christ of Latter Day Saints. Isn't that exciting!

CHAPTER 3

Let's Talk About the Book of Mormon

The coming forth of the Book of Mormon is foretold in Ezekial 37:16:

"Moreover, thou son of man, take thee one stick, and write upon it, For Judah, and for the children of Israel his companions; then take another stick, and write upon it, For Joseph, the stick of Ephraim, and for all the house of Israel his companions:"

"Stick" refers to their writing materials. They use the inner part of the papyrus plant, found along rivers, especially the Nile, to make a paper to write on. Then they wrapped it around a stick and thus the writings were referred to as a stick or scroll.

"Judah" refers to the tribe of Judah, which the Bible is primarily a history of the House of Judah. Joseph refers to the Book of Mormon because the Brass Plates of Laban revealed to Lehigh, the first prophet in the Book of Mormon, that he was of the lineage of Joseph or the House of Joseph.

The reaction to the coming forth of the Book of Mormon was foretold by the Lord through one of its prophets in 2 Nephi 29: 3:

"And because my word shall hiss forth, many of the Gentiles shall say: A Bible! A Bible! We have a Bible, And there cannot be any more Bible:"

Then they will refer to such Scriptures as Revelations 22:18-19:

"For I testify unto every man that heareth the words of the prophecy of this book, if any man shall add unto these things, God shall add unto him the plagues that are written in the book: And if any man shall take away from the words of the book of this prophecy, God shall take away his part out of the book of life, and out of the holy city, and from the things which are written in this book."

A careful reading of the above will reveal that John was referring to the prophecies that were in his book, not to the total book he had written. Obviously, John would not presume to talk about the writings of other prophets and apostles and what we today call the New Testament or even the Bible. His book of Revelations has been placed at the end of the New New Testament not because it was the last book written, but because it refers to the future so much. According to Bible scholars,

John himself wrote 1, 2 & 3 John at least 10 years after he wrote the Book of Revelation which was completed in about 95 AD. In addition, the word Bible is from the Greek word "ta biblia" which literally means "the books" or the plural of book. We correctly refer to the Book of Matthew or the Book of John so John was referring to his own book and, more specifically, to the prophecies within that book. By the way, Moses gave the same warning in Deuteronomy 4:2 when he said,

"Ye shall not add unto the word which I command you, neither shall ye diminish ought (any) from it, that ye may keep the commandments of the Lord your God which I command you."

Four other thoughts should be considered lest we have a closed mind regarding additional scriptures:

1. John himself wrote at the last of the Book of John:

    """And there are also many other things which Jesus did, the which, if they should be written every one, I suppose that even the world itself could not contain the books that should be written. Amen" Do we have the right to say that these other things that Jesus did were unimportant or that they wouldn't help us? I don't think so!

2. The Lord gave the same instruction to Joseph Smith, Jr. In Doctrine and Covenants 20:35:

    "And we know that these things are true and according to the revelations of John, neither adding to, nor diminishing from the prophecies of his book, the holy Scriptures, or the revelations of God which shall come hereafter by the gift and power of the Holy Ghost, the voice of God, or the ministering of angels."

To understand what "these things" refers to, it is necessary for the reader to read the first 34 verses of the 20th section of the Doctrine and Covenants.

3. Paul put the keeping of an open mind regarding additional scripture (although he was not referring to additional Scriptures alone) very well in Philippians 4: 8:

" Finally, brethren, whatsoever things are true, whatsoever things are honest, whatsoever things are just, whatsoever things are pure, whatsoever things are lovely, whatsoever things are of good report; if there be any virtue and if there be any praise, think on these things."

4. The Lord put it best and very pointedly in 2 Nephi 29:8:

"Wherefore murmur ye, (which means to complain, belittle or scoff) because that ye shall receive more of my word? Know ye not that the testimony of two nations is a witness unto you that I am God, that I remember one nation like unto another? Wherefore, I speak the same words unto one nation like unto another." Then he goes on in verse 9 and says, "And I do this that I may prove unto many that I am the same yesterday, today, and forever; for my work is not yet finished; neither shall it be until the end of man." Can we limit God? If we do believe in a living God, should we not listen to His words through His prophets?

So now, hopefully, you can have an open mind to additional scriptures and with that same open mind, decide whether they are true as Paul admonished us.

CHAPTER 4

What Then Is the Purpose of the Book of Mormon?

1. To be a second witness that Jesus Is the Christ-2 Corinthians 13: 1:

   "In the mouth of two or three witnesses shall every word be established."

   This is Paul repeating the law as far as the Jews were concerned as stated in Deuteronomy 19:15: "at the mouth of two witnesses, or at the mouth of three witnesses, shall the matter be established."

2. The title page of the Book of Mormon states its purpose: Convincing of the Jew and Gentile that Jesus Is the Christ, manifesting Himself to all nations, not just to the House of Judah.

WHO WROTE IT?

The prophets named in it wrote it. Mormon and his son, Moroni, abridged it. Joseph Smith, Jr translated it by the gift and power of God.

HOW DO WE KNOW? First, we must read it with an open mind. Then there are three methods by which we can learn if the Book of Mormon is true. First are the archaeological evidences, second is the witnesses and third is through prayer.

CHAPTER 5

Archaeological Evidences

Here are some things mentioned in the Book of Mormon, some of which are not widely accepted even today as to their existence prior to Cortez coming in 1519. No writer nor group of writers would have put them in the Book of Mormon in the 1820s or 1830s if they were simply writing the book because they didn't know of their existence!.The very first published report of archeological findings in Ancient America was published in 1841 in England, 11 years after the publishing of the Book of Mormon. So, here are some of those things.

1. Steel, iron, brass (mentioned in Jarom 1:8, 1 Nephi 4, 2 Nephi 5, Ether 10) Americas Ancient Civilizations, Page 82 says, "Even Indians, who possess far more patience and perseverance than white men, cannot carve diorite, arsenite or jasper with stone tools. While excavating the

ancient remains at Cocle in Panama I selected a plain piece of diorite that had been cut and squared by the long-vanished people and upon the surface I outlined a simple pattern. I provided five of my Indian workers with several dozen stone implements taken from the graves. I told them to cut the design on the stone. For 10 days they labored steadily. They completely wore out practically all of the stone implements yet they had not succeeded in producing any recognizable carving on the diorite."

Yet the long-vanished people had produced intricate carvings in diorite and harder stones. How did they do it? With steel instruments as the Book of Mormon says. Have any been found? Yes, they exist today in museums in Central and South America.

2. Wheels (Mentioned in 2 Nephi 15:28, Alma 18:9-10, 3 Nephi 21:14). For over 100 years, scientists would not credit the Ancient Americans with the knowledge of wheels. (In fact as a youth, I, Glenn Orr, was taught that they didn't have the wheel. The first I heard about it was in the Mesa Visitor's Center in that film which really shocked me!) Now such evidence of toys with wheels and huge stone wheels, some measuring over 8 feet in diameter, have been found.

3. Elephants (Mentioned in Ether 9:19) Found in the LaBrea Tar Pits, Los Angeles California. Calculated by

geologists to be at least 10,000 years ago in the middle or last of the Pleistocene Age. The La Brea Tar Pits were first discovered in the early 1900s with the first archaeological dig occurring in 1906. The bones of elephants have also been found in the Lost River area of Idaho in the middle 1900s.

4. Horses and cattle (mentioned in 1 Nephi 18:25, Enos 1:21, Alma 18:9-12, Ether 9:18-19) . They too have been found in the La Brea Tar Pits. Also, The National Geographic Society reported of an expedition that found entire horses, cattle, lions and tigers entrapped in glaciers in the Ice Age and they dated them to approximately 6000 years ago. This discovery was made in the 1980s, as I recall. In the January, 1981 issue of the National Geographic Magazine, they report of a find of horses and rhinoceroses entrapped in the volcanic ash deposited from a volcanic fallout that had smothered many of the above. This find was near Orchard, Nebraska, a small town in north central Nebraska. The volcanic cloud, which may have come hundreds of miles, was estimated to be hundreds of times larger than Mount St. Helena's volcanic cloud. It was estimated to have occurred about 12,000 years ago. In the September 1979 issue of the same magazine, it reports on a find near Clovis, New Mexico. There they found that, "The Clovis people downed and butchered elephants, horses and bison about 12,000 years ago." According to the

article, they were such excellent hunters that by the time Cortez came in 1519 that these animals, except for the bison, were extinct.

5. <u>Massive buildings, many of which are called temples, with intricate stone carvings</u>. These are all over Central and South America. This is referred to by the abridger and prophet Mormon (after whom the Book of Mormon is entitled) in Mormon 1:7,

"The whole face of the land had become covered with buildings, and the people were as numerous almost as it were the sand of the sea." They used to say that Central America was dotted with small hills but now they know that under the tropical vegetation are hundreds of buildings.

6. <u>Highways</u> (mentioned 3 Nephi 6:8) in America's Ancient Civilization it says ,"In some ways the greatest engineering feat of these people was the so-called Incan (Lamanite) road. Over 4,000 miles in length, it stretched from Quito in Ecuador to Tucuman Central Chile and traversed some of the roughest, most mountainous country in the world. There were ranges 14 to 15,000 feet in height to be scaled, vast canyons thousands of feet in depth to be crossed, roaring torrents to be bridged. Roman roads, proverbial for their permanence, have disappeared, and can be traced today only with difficulty, or not at all. Our modern roads will,

according to experts, if left to the forces of nature, have completely disappeared, without leaving a trace in 500 years, but this great Maya Road has withstood the passage of centuries, in a country of heavy rainfall and luxuriant vegetation, and with the exception of its cement facing, is almost the same now it was as it was the day when the last Maya trod its smooth level surface." (Ancient Cities and Modern Tribes, Gann p. 114)

7. <u>A wall or fortification from the East wilderness to the west sea near the River Sidon.</u> (Mentioned in Alma 50:11) Some 40 miles of the wall were found in 1932 in Peru along the north side of the Santa River in the Andes Mountain by the National Geographic Society and published in their January 1933 issue. Why the north side? That fits perfectly with the Book of Mormon account. The Nephites built the wall and occupied the land to the north. They would naturally want to force the Lamanites who occupied the land to the south to cross the river to reach the fortifications so they could shoot at them in the open. The wall in some places is 30 feet high and 15 feet thick at its base. You will note the difference in the name of the river. If you study history you will find name changes for the same place, river or town are very common.

These are but a few of the archaeological evidences of the Book of Mormon. I will mention a few more:

Are the Mormons Teaching Fables

1. In the book, Americans page 21 by Jordan (All sources quoted are non–Mormon except where noted) it says, "The best authorities agree that no human race is indigenous (started from the caveman) to the New World. Every human being that has ever lived in America has been an immigrant or the descendent of an immigrant."

   The Book of Mormon tells how they came here and from where they came. Years ago while I was in Mexico on a business trip, I talked with an archaeologist regarding his findings and I asked him if he had read the account of these people in the Book of Mormon. He answered that he had and that it no doubt was a history of the Mayan and Premayan people. I asked him if he was a member. No was the answer. Why? "Because there are too many angels for me!", he said. He didn't believe in the Bible either.

2. These people who did come were a very advanced people in architecture and astronomy. In fact, in an article in the Popular Science magazine, Spinden says, "With records cut in imperishable stone the Mayas suddenly made their appearance upon the historical scene on August 6, 613 BC. Where were the Mayas on August 5? Nobody Knows."

   The Book of Mormon tells where they are from and ties in perfectly with this article as to their time of departure and arrival.

3. Christopher Columbus said, "These people (referring to the people he discovered in the Caribbean) are of the Royal House of Jerusalem. (Life of Christopher Columbus Vol. 12, p 2) The Book of Mormon confirms that this is correct.

4. DeRoo, an American and a devout Catholic, wanting to clean up the record of the decadent Pope Alexander VI, went to the Vatican in the early 1900s. He knew ancient Latin and as he delved into the Secret Archives of the Vatican, he authored a much more exciting venture, "History of America before Columbus." Here Is what the priests who accompanied Cortez in 1519 found that the "Indians" believed:

"They believed in one God; they believed that this God had sent His son to the earth by a virgin; they believed that the son was killed on a tree; they believe that in three days he got up; They believed in baptism, the sacrament, resurrection, a likeness of heaven and hell, and that we would be judged by the kind of life we had lived as to which we will go. This led DeRoo to state,

"We trust that no intelligent reader would contradict us, if we should consider it sufficiently demonstrated that the Christian religion was preached in America during the first centuries of our era." Page 582. His statement is confirmed and clarified by the Book of Mormon.

There are many more, such as a confirmed archaeological fact that there was on this continent a light and a dark skinned people and that the dark race had the light race in subjection, all confirmed by the Book of Mormon. In addition to all these complexities, Joseph Smith was an unlearned man with a third grade formal education who, according to his wife, Emma, a schoolteacher, couldn't at the time of his translation of the Book of Mormon, dictate a good letter, much less something so complex as the Book of Mormon. I have seen some of his earlier letter writing and it is definitely as she said.

I hope you realize by now, just based on the evidences alone, that no man nor the best scientific minds grouped together could have written the Book of Mormon. The information did not exist on the earth in the 1820s to write such a complex book! By the way, to accurately translate the Book of Mormon from English to Spanish (Which are very similar languages) it took 5 to 6 scholars almost 3 years. It took Joseph 65 days to translate from reformed Egyptian to English (two very different languages). It had to be by the gift and power of God! But that is not all. We can now go to the second method.

CHAPTER 6

Truthfulness of the Witnesses

You know, our whole system of justice revolves around the HONESTY AND INTEGRITY OF WITNESSES. People are judged by a jury of their peers to be guilty or innocent by the testimony of witnesses. What the jury must decide is whether the witnesses are reliable, are they honest, do they have integrity? Will they change their story under cross-examination? Why then can't we use the same rationale to decide whether the Book of Mormon is true or not? Of course we can, and we can judge for ourselves how the witnesses reacted to cross-examination.

The whole concept of RELIABLE WITNESSES Is age-old and has stood the test of time. The word witness is first referred to by Abraham in Genesis 21:30. Then it is used in the Ten Commandments when it says, "Thou shalt not bear false witness against thy neighbor." (Exodus 20:16) One witness will not convict as stated in Numbers 35:30 and Deuteronomy 17:6. That Is why Joseph Smith's witness alone is not sufficient. This is clarified in Deuteronomy 19:15-18 that two or three witnesses are needed and it is repeated by Paul in 2 Corinthians 13:1. Because of all this it became known as the Law of Witnesses.

The Law of Witnesses was certainly believed and practiced by the Book of Mormon people. Since their genealogy goes back to Joseph, the son of Jacob, this is perfectly logical. An example of the Law is found in the 9th and 10th chapters of Alma. They didn't believe Alma (Alma 9:6) until Amulek testified.

Also in 10:12: "And now when Amulek had spoken these words the people began to be astonished, saying there was more than one witness who testified of the things whereof they were accused, and also other things which were to come, according to the spirit of prophecy which was in them."

To emphasize the importance of the word "witness", it or its derivatives is used 307 times in the Scriptures. So, let's take a look at the Book of Mormon witnesses.

There were, in addition to Joseph, three witnesses to which the Angel Moroni testified. See their statement at the beginning of the Book of Mormon. Then there were eight more. Read their statement as well. Obviously, the Lord knew how like Doubting Thomas we are as a people to have 11 witnesses! All three, Oliver Cowdery, David Whitmer, and Martin Harris, left

TRUTHFULNESS OF THE WITNESSES

the church and felt that Joseph was a "fallen prophet." Yet they never denied the Book of Mormon and in fact went to great lengths to let everyone know that the angel had appeared to them in the brightness of day. Why?

Wouldn't the logical thing for them to do (even if they had seen an angel as they claimed) would be to deny it to "get even" as many of the Antis "cross-examined" them and encouraged them to do? Why didn't they? Part of the reason can be found in Proverbs 19:9 where it says, "A false witness shall not be unpunished and he that speaketh lies shall perish. They didn't because they had seen an angel approximately at noon and the angel had told them there would be no peace for them in this life or the life to come if they ever denied it!

Also, if these men had seen the angel and the plates, how could they permit themselves to leave the Church? Good question. The specifics vary but the fundamental answer is that those who had received such special favor had special problems with egotism.

If anyone could expose Joseph as a fraud it would be Oliver Cowdery so we should look at this witness the closest. Oliver was the scribe for Joseph when Joseph translated the entire Book of Mormon, "but a few pages," says Oliver in his statement made in the winter of 1848 when he was rebaptized at Council Bluffs, Iowa. He was the second witness with Joseph when they received the Aaronic and then the Melchizedek

Priesthood. He re-wrote the first copy of the Book of Mormon from his original writing when he was taking dictation from Joseph and they slipped the second copy by night to the typesetter In Palmyra. So, from 1829 to 1838, Oliver was the most important man in the Church after Joseph. He was given the title of First Assistant or Second Elder and was higher in authority than Joseph's counselors.

So, why did he leave the Church? Probably jealousy over the association of Sidney Rigdon and Joseph as Sidney helped Joseph with the clarification of many passages in the Bible. Oliver then became involved with the Whitmer Brothers-as he married their sister-in land sales to the Saints in Missouri in which they made quite a bit of money off the markup. Specifically, the charge was that Oliver had acted as an attorney in suing some of the Saints for payments on their land they had purchased. He was excommunicated April 12, 1838.

Oliver became an attorney after he left the Church. On one occasion he faced a cross-examination when an opposing attorney accosted him in court with the accusation that he was one of those Mormons who had testified and written that he had beheld an angel of God! Rather than denying it or getting flustered, as the opposing attorney hoped, he responded, "Whatever my faults and weaknesses might be, the testimony which I had written in which I gave to the world, was literally true." Oliver never varied from his testimony and in spite of being away from the Church for ten years he never denied what he had seen as a witness. Many statements are found in the records regarding his honesty and integrity. He died in 1850 of pneumonia, thought to be brought on by tuberculosis.

In 1833 David Whitmer faced one of his many cross-examinations. A mob of some 500 men cornered him and other leaders in the public square in Independence, Missouri. They proceeded to strip them, then tar and feather them, a very painful torture that sometimes resulted in the death of the one tarred and feathered. Then the commanding officer called 12 men to be a firing squad. He then threatened the men with death if they did not deny the Book of Mormon. If they did they would welcome them as Citizens. David Whitmer raised his hands, bore his witness that the Book of Mormon was the Word of God. The mob was so shaken they let him and the others go. One doctor present, an unbeliever, joined the Church because of David's fearless testimony in the face of certain death.

David was excommunicated on April 13, 1838, one day after Oliver. He expressed years later his feelings that Sidney Rigdon had come between him and Joseph. David was thought of so highly by some of the Saints that there was a move on to depose Joseph and replace him with David because of the downfall of the Kirtland Safety Society, a bank formed by members of the Church including Joseph. Joseph had resigned from the bank because he thought the leaders were too speculative but because he had prophesied that someday the banknotes would be on a par with gold and the bank failed, he was a "fallen prophet" in their critical eyes. (This prophecy was fulfilled in Utah in 1847, three years after the death of Joseph.)

Some 47 years later in 1880, David was a respected businessman in Richmond, Missouri. A nearby agnostic, John Murphy, published a report that David had denied the truthfulness of the Book of Mormon. Again, David had to face cross-examination. David took out a full-page ad and he had 22 respected business and professional leaders sign a statement that they had known him for 40 years as a man of the highest integrity. He then said he had never denied the angel nor the Book of Mormon. None on the list publicly accepted the Book of Mormon but all admired David Witmer for his integrity. He died in 1888, never having rejoined the Church, but never denying his witness. Wow!

Even in "Mormonism Unveiled", an anti–Mormon and really a libelous book published in 1834, Martin Harris is depicted as an "honest, industrious citizen". Martin ultimately sold part of his farm to pay for the publishing of the Book of Mormon. He did many great works but did not leave Kirtland when the rest went to Nauvoo. He used to say, "The Church left me-I didn't leave the Church." In 1846, Martin Harris went to England on behalf of the apostate group, the Strangites. He was asked to speak at a Birmingham Conference of the Church Of Jesus Christ Of Latter Day Saints and was publicly repudiated by the presiding officer. He angrily left the meeting and many Antis were outside, fully expecting to hear him disclaim Mormonism. In his cross-examination he said, "Do you know that the sun is shining? (The sun was shining so of course they knew it.) Because as sure as you know that, I know that Joseph Smith was a true prophet of God and that he translated that book by the power of God." He described the plates as 6 x 8 inches and about 4 inches thick, weighing about 40-60 pounds, two thirds of them being sealed. (I saw the wooden lap-top desk in which the plates were kept by Joseph. The Patriarch of the Church-now emeritus-Eldred G Smith, has it in his possession and displays it around the United States. The plates plus the rings could only be about 6 inches high.) Martin later said he "dare not deny it" when he was 92. He died in 1875, being almost daily cross-examined, always testifying to the truthfulness, never varying.

What about the eight witnesses who were shown the plates? Four were the Whitmer Brothers plus Hiram Page, their brother-in-law. All were considered men of integrity. All five left the Church or were excommunicated. It was said of them, "In fellowship or alienation, youth or age, persecution, poverty or affluence, the four Whitmer Brothers and Hiram Page never altered their plain testimony that they handled the original metal record of the Book of Mormon."

That leaves the three Smiths, Joseph Smith, Sr., (Joseph's father) Hiram Smith and Samuel Smith-Joseph's brothers. They never left Joseph. On one occasion, Joseph Smith, Sr. was offered freedom if he would renounce the Book of Mormon. Since he would not he was starved for four days and jailed for 30 more.

So the integrity of the 11 witnesses stood the toughest kinds of cross-examination, many times in the face of death and defamation. It alone should convince many as to the truthfulness of the Book of Mormon and certainly, coupled with the archaeological evidences, should convince all men and women of good-will who have an open mind. However, there is one more method. It is prayer.

CHAPTER 7

Do We Need to Pray About It?

Frankly, this is the easiest method. Let's use only two main scriptures. Let's use James 1:5-6 and MoronI 10:3-5.

1. James 1:5 says,

    "If any of you lack wisdom, let him ask of God, that giveth to all men liberally, and upbraideth not; and it shall be given him." Now, many ask but they forget this sixth verse: "But let him ask in faith, nothing wavering. For he that wavereth is like a wave of the sea driven with the wind and tossed." In other words, no answer will come without faith.

2. There is further clarification in Moroni 10: 3-5: "Behold, I would exhort (encourage) you that when ye shall read these things and ponder (pray and then study) it in your hearts, and when ye shall receive these things, I would

exhort you that ye would ask God, the Eternal Father, in the name of Christ, if these things are not true; and if you shall ask with a sincere heart, with real intent, having faith in Christ, he will manifest the truth of it unto you, by the power of the Holy Ghost. And by the power of the Holy Ghost ye may know the truth of all things."

So now, when we put all things together we must 1. Read; 2 study after prayer; 3 ask; 4 be sincere; 5 have real intent: (Real intent means to have the willingness to accept the answer and make whatever changes in your life are necessary. In this case to clean up our life if necessary, be baptized and so live our life to go to the Holy Temple.) 6. Have faith in Christ and the answer will come.

Okay, so how do I recognize the answer? Paul gives us a great way when he explains in Galatians 5:22-23 how the Holy Ghost answers: "But the fruit of the Spirit (Holy Ghost) is love, joy, peace, long-suffering, gentleness, goodness, faith, and 23. Meekness, temperance; against such there is no law."

"Against such there is no law" means there is no law limiting these wonderful feelings and neither can Satan prevent them if we are obedient. When I have answers to my prayers, there is such a feeling of peace, joy and I get a tingling sensation that runs down my spine. I do not get the "burning in my bosom"as the Lord told Oliver Cowdery D&C 9:7-9. I used to feel something was wrong with me until I heard Elder Boyd J Packer of the Twelve Apostles say that he hadn't either. He instead has strong feelings of peace. On one occasion about six months ago the feeling was as if a voice had said to me,"It's okay". Hopefully, by telling you how I have had prayers answered it will help you.

Yes, the Book of Mormon is true. I add my humble witness to it. No man nor group of men could have written it in the 1800s. It is what Joseph said it is. We are so fortunate to have it. Study it, then heed and do and you will have feelings of great joy to know you are on the right path to Eternal Life and Exaltation to be with Heavenly Father and Jesus Christ again. However, I also leave this warning with you from the Book of Mormon: (Mormon 9:7-9)

7. "And again I speak unto you who deny the revelations of God, and say that they are done away, that there are no revelations, nor prophecies, nor gifts, nor healing, nor speaking with tongues, and the interpretation of tongues;

8. Behold I say unto you, he that denieth these things knoweth not the gospel of Christ; yea, he has not read the Scriptures; if so, he does not understand them.

9. For do we not read that God is the same yesterday, today, and forever, and in him there is no variableness neither shadow of changing?"

Then these final words from the great prophet, Nephi (2 Nephi 33:10-11)

10. "And now, my beloved brethren, and also Jew, and all ye ends of the earth, hearken unto these words and believe in Christ; and if ye believe not in these words believe in Christ. And if ye shall believe in Christ ye will believe in these words, for they are the words of Christ, and he has given them unto me; and they teach all men that they should do good.

11. And if they are not the words of Christ, judge ye for Christ will show unto you, with power and great glory, that they are his words, at the last day; and you and I shall stand face to face before his bar; and ye shall know that I have been commanded of him to write these things, notwithstanding my weaknesses."

In other words, don't scoff or take lightly the Book of Mormon and the Church of Jesus of Latter Day Saints but examine it carefully with an open mind. The last day referred to is the Day of Judgment.

Please don't wait until the last day to find out the truth. Use the three methods above so that you may also find out that the Book of Mormon is true and that The Church of Jesus Christ of Latter Day Saints has been restored to the earth for the ushering in of the Millennium. What great peace, happiness and eternal joy is yours if you heed and do as He directs.

In the name of Jesus Christ, Amen.

Bibliography:

The Holy Scriptures

Encyclopedia of Mormonism

Mormon Doctrine by Bruce R McConkie

Investigating the Book of Mormon Witnesses by Richard Lloyd Anderson

The Americas before Columbus by Dewey Farnsworth

Book of Mormon evidences in ancient America by Dewey Farnsworth

Christ in ancient America by Milton R Hunter

America's Ancient Civilization by A. Hyatt Verrill

CHAPTER 8

How Did a French Word Get in the Book of Mormon? Jacob 7:27

Some Anti's have made a big thing out of Jacob using this word to say "goodbye" and "God Bless You" in the same words. They say the French language was not developed until hundreds of years after Jacob's time. True. Neither was the English language developed until hundreds of years later! Obviously, Jacob spoke neither in English nor French! Get real!

The translator, Joseph Smith, Jr., used it, not Jacob. "Adieu" means more than "goodbye" as it literally means "To God" short for "Go with God" or "Travel with God" or "God Bless You As You Travel." If Joseph had known the Spanish word, "Adios" he might have used it instead. It conveys the exact same meaning. However, there was very little, if any, Spanish influence in Western New York in the early 1800's. On the other hand, French fur traders had been coming to Western New York for over a hundred years and their influence was definite.

The Hebrew word, "Lebitra'ot"-or an abbreviated form thereof-conveys the same meaning (a goodbye with a blessing rather than a simple goodbye) and would be more likely the word used on the plates. The reason I say "or an abbreviated form thereof" is revealed in Mormon 9:32-33 where it states that the reformed Egyptian was a shorthand version of Hebrew. When you consider that two pages of Hebrew takes fifteen pages of English for the translation from Hebrew to English, you can see the reformed Egyptian must have really been an abbreviated language! Hopefully you can see from this that the Anti's are up to their old tricks-mix a little bit of truth with shallow or false logic. That is why we must have prophets and apostles to lead us so, as Paul says, "That we henceforth be no more children, tossed to and fro, and carried about with every wind of doctrine, by the sleight of men, and cunning craftiness, whereby they lie in wait to deceive." Ephesians 4:14 See also D&C 123:12.

Bibliography: Book of Mormon Student Manual-Religion 121 and 122 Standard Works

CHAPTER 9

Is the Book of Mormon True?

Is the Book of Mormon true? Is this the greatest work to be revealed to Man in the 19th and twentieth centuries by the Lords servants? If it is what it claims to be-a second witness that Jesus is the Messiah-then Joseph Smith Jr., the translator, is a true prophet of God as surely as Moses, Elijah, Isaiah, Peter and Paul were. If Joseph is a true prophet of God, then all his successors are true prophets of God. If Joseph is a true prophet of God, then the Church of Jesus Christ of Latter Day Saints (called Latter to distinguish it from the Former, set up in Christ's time) is the correct Church to which we should belong today. If some claim that it is the greatest work of the 19th and 20th centuries, then it is of paramount importance for each of us to find out if the Book of Mormon is true. We must not take it lightly nor give it a scan reading nor take the word of detractors who have done the same.

CHAPTER 10

A Catholic Priest Comments on the Book of Mormon

After reading about just one evidence of the truthfulness of the book of Mormon, a Dutch Catholic, Father J.R. Nijmegen, said in 1982:

"I wish that all my colleague-priests could read this remarkable article. It was a revelation for me. I have several inexpensive articles and books on my desk that give a "quick" explanation of Mormonism. The Book of Mormon is there noted as both "gruff and mixed", "styleless", and a "caricature of the Bible,"and "heathenish and disordered."

And now it appears that this Book is built on rich and perfect chiastic structures, which places it as an authentic literary document on the same high plain as the best texts from Biblical antiquity. I think that students and critics of the Mormon Church must learn to be more objective and careful in their judgments. Whoever would dispatch the Book of Mormon with a few cheap statements only shows that the spirit of the Inquisition is not yet dead! The Book of Mormon is an intriguing book. We must be able to and dare to judge it for its internal value."

In a pamphlet entitled The Strength of the Mormon Position, Elder Orson F Whitney, of the Council of the Twelve Apostles (1906-1931), related the following incident under the heading:

CHAPTER 11

You Mormons Are All Ignoramuses!

"Many years ago a learned man, a member of the Roman Catholic Church, came to Utah and spoke from the stand of the Salt Lake Tabernacle. I became well acquainted with him and we conversed freely and frankly. A great scholar, with perhaps a dozen languages at his tongue's end, he seemed to know all about theology, law, literature, science and philosophy. One day he said to me: "**You Mormons Are All Ignoramuses.** You don't even know the strength of your own position. It is so strong that there is only one other tenable (position) in the whole Christian world, and that is the position of the Catholic Church. The issue is between Catholicism and Mormonism. If we are right, you are wrong; if you are right, we are wrong; and that's all there is to it. The Protestants haven't a leg to stand on. For, if we are wrong, they are wrong with us, since they were a part of us and went out from us, while if we are right, they are apostates whom we cut off long ago. If we have the apostolic succession from St. Peter, as we claim, there is no need of Joseph Smith and Mormonism; but if we have not that succession, then such a man as Joseph Smith was necessary, and Mormonism's attitude is the only consistent one. It is either the perpetuation of the gospel from ancient times, or the restoration of the gospel in latter days."

More and more evidence of the truthfulness of the Book of Mormon keeps coming to light. President Packer, acting President of the Twelve Apostles, said recently that he thinks the Lord is letting these evidences surface to strengthen the members in these last days. In chapters 5 & 6, I mentioned two of them: Law of Witnesses and the Archeolocical Evidences. In this chapter I would like to mention some others:

1. The route Lehi describes that they took in their exodus from Jerusalem fits perfectly with an ancient trade route not rediscovered until the 1900s.

2. A repetitive form of writing was discovered and became generally accepted in 1942 to exist in the Bible. It is a style of writing used in the Old Testament called Chiasmus. Since the Book of Mormon encompasses much of the same time. Then, if it is authentic, it should have the same style of writing. Does it?

3. By their frequency of usage of the "filler" (also called non-contextual) words-such as a, and, the, that, too, for,

of, in, this, now and be-authors leave their linguistic fingerprints or word prints on their manuscripts as surely as we leave our individual fingerprints. This, with the aid of the computer, has become a science called stylometry. They can factually tell us who did or did not write something. Amazing! Then, who did write the Book of Mormon and who did not?

4. One of those "cheap statements" that Father Nijmegen refers to from the Antis is that "American sentiments (politics, form of government and revolution) permeate the work," With the conclusion that the Book of Mormon was written in the 19th century. Is this a true conclusion?

CHAPTER 12

Exodus from Jerusalem

Lehi, in chapters 16-17, of 1 Nephi describes a route across the near barren desert of Southern Arabia as on this map.

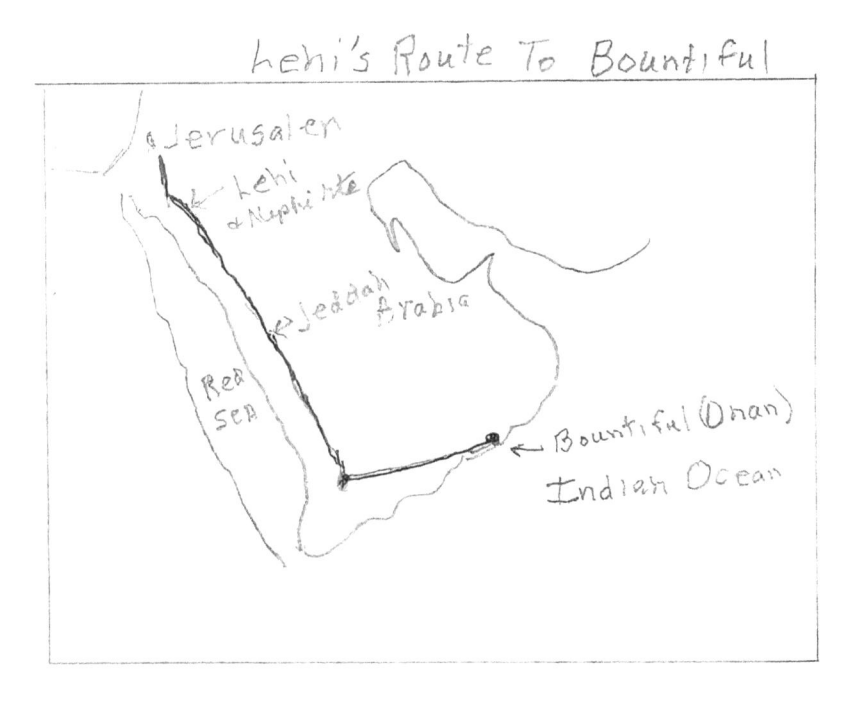

We need to ask ourselves two questions:

A. In light of today's knowledge of geography, was this route a plausible one?

B. Could Joseph Smith-or any man or group of men in the 1820s-have known in the United States of a route such as this?

A PLAUSIBLE ROUTE?

Not only was it plausible, it was probably the only route through which such a caravan could travel and survive in this very barren country. Modern research has recovered knowledge of an ancient caravan route called The Frankincense Trail which leads from Dhofar, in today's Oman, the ancient source of that precious material, to near Jerusalem that conforms in detail to Nephi's account. It goes from Dhofar almost due west to the Red Sea and then north-northwest "near" the Red Sea to Jerusalem. Evidently it was known well in Lehi's time.

Nephi broke his bow (1 Nephi 16:18) and the bows of the brothers lost their spring. (1 Nephi 16:21). This would be caused by a place of very high humidity. How could this happen in a desert where there is very low humidity? Jeddah, midway down the Western shore of the Red Sea, is known for a combination of heat, humidity, sand and salt that rusts car fenders in a few months and turns limber any dry wood brought from other areas! Around Jeddah grows the pomegranate tree, excellent for bow making so there was a right wood available for making a new bow. Then nearby even in today there are "wild beasts" in the mountains-wild asses, gazelles, grouse, partridge, etc., which are still hunted with slings. (1 Nephi 16:23, 31)

They spent about eight years getting to the Arabian Sea and came to a place they called Bountiful which was a luxurious place, a huge oasis where there were huge trees suitable for ship building. This was not known to exist until in the 1920s and then only by the explorers. In addition, there are favorable trade winds to launch a ship to the west.

In 1996 a video entitled, **From Jerusalem to the Land of Promise,** Arthur J Kocherhans uses the tradewinds and Nephi's description to find where they actually landed. He uses 1 Nephi 18:24 to show that it has to be a climate similar to the Mediterranean climate of Jerusalem because the seeds grew "exceedingly". Only three areas qualified that had a westerly trade wind and a Mediterranean climate. They are the southern coast of Australia, the southern tip of Africa and the Western central part of Chile in South America. Nephi further qualifies the area by saying that there was gold, silver and copper. (1 Nephi 18:24) . The only one of those three areas, according to the World Book of Encyclopedia, that has all three is the Western central area of Chile.

These are just a few of the tangible evidences of the correctness of the Book of Mormon but let's go on.

CHAPTER 13

Could Anyone in the United States Have Known of It in 1829?

Eugene Anglin, Ph.D, Associate Professor of English at Brigham Young University, did an exhaustive search into the literature available in the 1820s and 1830s. What information was available was misinformation and that it was not correct. Conder's Arabia (London, 1825) describes the whole southern coastline of Arabia as "a rocky wall… as dismal and barren as can be; not a blade of grass or a green thing." As late as the 1920s Explorer Bartram Thomas was surprised at the thickly wooded wadis of Dhofar which corresponds to the location of Bountiful. Conclusion: Not even the English explorers knew that there was a luxurious area fitting the description of Bountiful (1 Nephi 17:5-6), much less a 24-year-old with third grade education in Western New York in 1829!

CHAPTER 14

Chiasmus

This is an ancient style of writing which aids in memorization because the thoughts are repeated in reverse order. Although discovered by John Forbes in 1854 in his Symmetrical Structures of Scriptures, it was not until 1942 that it became generally accepted, having been lost for centuries. It was found in many places in the Old Testament. "Chi" in the Greek alphabet is written as an X and that is the way they are diagrammed- at least the left side of the X. For example, selecting keywords and translating them from the Hebrew, Genesis 7:21-23 is diagrammed as follows:

      a. There died on the earth
        b. all birds
          c. cattle
            d. beasts and creeping things

      e. man
       f. all life
        g. died
        g' and was destroyed
       f' Every living thing
      e' both man
     d' creeping things
    c' cattle
   b' birds
a' were destroyed from the earth

There are many of these in the Old Testament such as Leviticus 24:13-23, Psalms 3:7-8, Psalms 58, Isaiah 60:1-3 and in the New Testament in Matthew 13:13-18. So if the Book of Mormon is from a similar time period then there should be a Chiasmus in it. There is! We have diagrammed two-1 Nephi 21:1 and Alma 36-. Also, 1 Nephi 15:9-11, 17:36-39, 2 Nephi 25:24-27, 29:13, Mosiah 3:18-19, 5:10-12 and Alma 41:13-15 to name a few. There are also long ones in Lehi's account in 1 Nephi chapters 1-9 and Nephi's account. 1 Nephi chapters 10-22. What does all this mean? It is further evidence that the Book of Mormon was written by the prophets in a manner of writing not known in the 1820s by the scholars, much less by an unlearned or illiterate young man, as Prof. Hugh Nibley calls Joseph. This is also the evidence referred to by Father Nijmegen.

CHAPTER 15

Wordprint

By their frequency of usage of the "filler" (also called non contextual) words-such as a, and, the, that, to, for, of, in, this, now and be-authors leave their linguistic fingerprints or word prints on their manuscripts as surely as we leave our individual fingerprints. This, with the aid of the computer, has become a science called stylometry. They can factually tell us who did or did not write something. Then, who did write the Book of Mormon and who did not?

Two statisticians, Wayne A Larson, PhD, and Alvin C Rencher PhD, report their findings in the book, Book of Mormon Authorship. They examined the known writings of Joseph Smith, Solomon Spalding and Sidney Rigdon who Antis have said that they wrote it rather than Joseph translating it. They also examined the known writings of Church prophets named in the Book of Mormon plus the words attributed to Jesus, Lord and Father. They used three statistical techniques: Multivariate Analysis of Variance, Cluster Analysis and Discriminate or Classification Analysis. They came to the following conclusions:

1. The statistical odds that a single author wrote the Book of Mormon are 100 billion to 1 against it..

2. There is some evidence of a wordprint <u>time trend</u> within the Book of Mormon; i.e., Writers are more similar to their contemporaries than to writers in other time periods.

3. None of the Book of Mormon selections resembled the writing of any of the suggested 19 century authors mentioned above including Joseph Smith!

4. The statistical probability of #2 and #3 of being inaccurate are one in 10 billion.

5. It does not seem possible that Joseph Smith or any other writer could have falsified a work in the styles of 24 authors separately, keeping the frequency of use of the 38 filler words individualistic to the author. And remember, the authors are intermixed frequently.

6. The implications for translation are that the process was both direct and literal and that each individual author's style was preserved. Apparently Joseph Smith was required to render the book in a rather precise format with minimum deviations from the original wordprint.

What does all this mean? It means that we now have a scientific and measurable means to prove the Book of Mormon is not authored in the 1820s and that it is not authored by one man but by several men.

CHAPTER 16

The Anti's Claim It Was Written in the Nineteenth Century

One of those "cheap statements" that Father Nijmegen refers to is that "American sentiments of politics, former government and revolution permeate the work", With the conclusion that the Book of Mormon was written in the 19th century. This was authored by Thomas O'Dea and quoted without verification by other anti–Mormon writers. Is this true?

Here was the political fervor of the 1820s in the United States:

1. The depiction of the American Revolution as heroic resistance against tyranny;
2. The belief that people overthrow their kings under the stimulus of enlightened ideas of human rights;

3. The conviction that constitutional arrangements such as frequent election, separation of powers, and popularly elected assemblies were necessary to control power.

In 1 Nephi 13:17-19 Nephi prophesies regarding the Revolutionary War,

"And I beheld that their mother Gentiles were gathered together upon the waters, and upon the land also, to battle against them. And I beheld that the power of God was with them, and also that the wrath of God was upon all those that were gathered together against them to battle. And I, Nephi, beheld that the Gentiles that had gone out of captivity were delivered by the power of God out of the hands of all other nations."

There is no indictment of the king or parliament, no reference to American resistance. God, not Gen. Washington, delivered the colonies. If we remember the history of that war, we remember that Washington's Army Was Ill-fed and ill-clothed for the winter at Valley Forge and soldiers were deserting daily. It was only by God's deliverance that they were able to surprise the British and defeat them. Gen. Washington was the first to agree.

1. The theme of deliverance by God is more notable in Nephi's prophecy because it recurs in various forms throughout the Book of Mormon. Three times a people

of God suffer from oppressive rulers under conditions that might approximate those in the colonies before the Revolution: Alma under King Noah, (Mosiah 18:34) the people of Limhi under the Lamanites, (Mosiah 22:11) and once again Alma under the Lamanites. (Mosiah 24:9, 13, 19-21, Alma 5:4-5) in each case the people escape from bondage by flight rather than revolution.

2. The belief that people overthrow their kings under the stimulus of enlightened ideas of human rights is not to be found in the Book of Mormon. On the contrary, the people wanted a King and It Was King Mosiah II who persuaded them to not have a king after his sons refused the kingship. (Mosiah 29)

3. The conviction that constitutional arrangements such as frequent election, separation of powers, and popularly elected assemblies were necessary to control power was not in evidence in the Book of Mormon. The Chief Judge much more resembled a king than an American president. There were no frequent elections (life tenure was enjoyed) and the Chief Judge usually appointed his successor. (Alma 4:16, 50:39, Helaman 1:13)

So, where is the "American sentiment that permeates the Book of Mormon"? It doesn't exist!

Now, let's summarize what we have learned:

1. The ancient law of the Law of Witnesses was clarified. The Three Witnesses and the Eight Witnesses, although separated from Joseph Smith and the Church, never denied their testimony.

2. Archaeological finds since the 1830s have substantiated many of the items such as steel and metal plates, horses, elephants etc., that are spoken of in the Book of Mormon which were unknown to exist in America in the 1830s. As a youth I was taught that the first horses were brought over by the Spanish Conquistadors.

3. The route that Lehi took on his exodus from Jerusalem could only be as it is described in the Book of Mormon. Otherwise they could not have made it to the Land of Promise or what later was called The New World.

4. The same style of writing found in the Old Testament but not generally recognized until 1942 called Chiasmus is also found in the Book of Mormon. This indicates that the Book of Mormon was actually written by people in the Old Testament time and not by any writer in the 1820s as this type of writing was unknown even by scholars in the 1820s.

5. We can now tell the authorship of a book by the science called Stylometry or word prints just as surely as we can be traced by our fingerprints. The odds of any one

person writing the Book of Mormon are in excess of 1 billion to 1 against it and of Joseph Smith to have written the Book of Mormon are even greater against it.

6. The Book of Mormon should not be taken nor dismissed lightly. It should be given daily, deep and personal study after prayer.

CHAPTER 17

Can You Duplicate It?

Let's use one final method of seeing if you can discredit the Book of Mormon, that of duplication. Here are the ground rules:

1. You must know nothing about the people.

2. You must present your book of over 500 pages to the world as a true work and not a work of fiction.

3. You must intertwine civilizations over a period of some 2000 years and that period of time to be over 2000 years ago.

4. You must tell about their culture including their government and their religion and it must become a second witness for Jesus Christ.

5. You must get 11 men of impeccable reputation, who would never lie, to say that your work is true. Then most of these men must renounce you and leave your organization but never deny the truthfulness of your book. Mind you, they can never make a penny off your book. In fact, it must cost some their livelihood.

6. You must write in the style of writing unknown today but to become known in 110 years from now as the style of writing of the people in that period.

7. You must present it not as your writing but as a translation with as many as 32 different styles of writing that can't be traced back to your style of writing by the science of Stylometry. You must claim that you are in the possession of thin gold plates from which you translate. You must move from place to place to hide from robbers who will try to steal the plates from you, using force if necessary.

8. You can prepare and study from the age of 14 when you first get the idea until you are 23. However, you can only go to the third grade and you must help support your family on the farm so there is precious little time for preparation.

9. Since you can't write very well, you must ask others to write it down for you by taking dictation from you. When dictating, you must never ask for the last words dictated to be repeated to you but must start where

you left off the last time you were dictating. You must dictate it without punctuation (periods, commas, paragraphs, etc.,) and hope that the typesetter can place the punctuation correctly.

10. You must do all this in approximately two months! It took as many as six scholars almost 3 years to translate the Book of Mormon from English to Spanish-two very similar and known languages.

IMPOSSIBLE! you say. I agree. Then there is only one position that is left. Joseph Smith translated the Book of Mormon by the gift and power of God to help Jew and Gentile to come unto Christ because of this Second Witness. Joseph Smith is a prophet of God as surely as Moses, Elijah, Isaiah, Peter and Paul are Prophets. The Church of Jesus Christ has been restored to the earth for you and me so that we might prepare everyone for the Millennium and the return to be in His presence.

We invite all to come to the restored truths. We don't say throw away all your old beliefs. Come and add to them the beautiful truths that have been given. It is exciting and fulfilling and it will feel right for you! This is the fastest growing church today. Why? Because it feels right. In this paper I can only cover a few of the evidences stated in the bibliography below. You can read them for more wonderful details.

BIBLIOGRAPHY:

F.A.R.M.S. Magazine, March 1983 (Foundation for Ancient Research and Mormon Studies)

Are You Mormons Ignoramuses? By Stephen G Morgan

Book of Mormon Authorship, Edited and compiled by Noel B Reynolds and published by F.A.R.M.S.

Book of Mormon Institute Manual by The Church Of Jesus Christ Of Latter Day Saints, 1981 Edition

Lehi in the Desert By Hugh Nibley

HOW DO WE RECOGNIZE A FALSE PROPHET & TEACHER?

1. 2 Peter 2:3 says, in talking about false prophets and teachers, "And through covetousness shall they with feigned words make merchandise of you:" In other words, in the last days, one way of spotting a false prophet or teacher is one who makes money by his preaching from the people he teaches. They are sometimes called "love offerings." They go around to churches, teaching against other churches, especially the Church of Jesus Christ of Latter Day Saints, which they label a "cult". See the chapter on Cults. It clearly points out that we are in good company because Jesus Christ and His gospel

teachings, in His day, definitely would be classified as a cult.

2. 2 Peter 2:12 says the false teachers and prophets will, "... speak evil of the things they understand not;.." So they will ridicule Gospel truths that they do not understand. Why do they ridicule?

   1. By doing so they make money. It is more profitable to tear down (look at the headlines in your newspaper-bad news sells papers!) than to build up and to state the positive.

   2. Why don't they understand? Same reason plus 1 Corinthians 2:14 Paul says, "But the natural man receiveth not the things of the Spirit of God: for they are foolishness unto him; neither can he know them, because they are spiritually discerned."

3. 2 Peter 2:14 says that the false prophets and teachers will, "Having eyes full of adultery, and that cannot cease from sin; beguiling unstable souls:...." Verse 19 says that they are in the bondage of sin.

4. Ephesians 2:20 says that the church is "...built upon the foundation of the apostles and prophets, Jesus Christ himself being the chief cornerstone;". Then, in the same letter to the Ephesians, in 4:11, Paul talks about apostles and prophets again and adds evangelists, pastors and teachers. <u>Why this heavy emphasis on having the proper organization and foundation of</u>

the church? Paul explains it in 4:14, "That we henceforth be no more children, tossed to and fro, and carried about with every wind of doctrine, by the sleight of men, and cunning craftiness, whereby they lie in wait to deceive." There is a series of books by that title, **THEY LIE IN WAIT TO DECEIVE**, exposing many of the more notorious anti-Mormons.

5. Why do they try to deceive us by their half-truths and, in some cases, by outright lies?

- Certainly 2 Peter 2:3 tells one reason-for money but it usually starts out for another reason:

- Jesus said in John 16:2, "They shall put you out of the synagogues: yea, the time cometh, that whosoever killeth you will think that he doeth God service." Certainly, we need look no further than the Book of Acts, Chapter 8 where it talks about the zealot Saul (Paul) who consented and was probably part of the Sanhedrin who were responsible for the stoning to death of Stephen. Paul, at that time, certainly felt he was doing God a service in getting rid of the cult who were becoming known as Christians.

- Certainly, many of the anti-Mormons-if they succeed in "killing" the testimony of a member-feel that they are doing God service. Many repeat half-truths or lies because they believe the credentials of the anti-Mormon who originated them without really checking them out.

6. A false prophet or teacher will teach other gospel than Paul taught, says Paul. See the chapter, ARE MORMONS TEACHING FABLES?. In Galatians 1:8, Paul taught that if you teach other than what he taught you would be accursed. <u>What did Paul teach?</u>

   - 1. God and Jesus Christ are separate personages, not just of spirit or essence or mist as stated in the Nicene Creed.
   - 2. Jesus Christ created this world and other worlds.
   - 3. There was a life before this life.
   - 4. Jesus atoned for our sins but we must do more than simply believe to regain his presence. Saying, "I believe" is not enough.
   - 5. Baptism by immersion.
   - 6. Proper organization of the Church.
   - 7. Gift of tongues, etc.
   - 8. Unpaid ministry. Must take care of the poor. We must not forbid marriage.
   - 9. Three degrees of glory. Resurrection for all.
   - 10. Must have the authority to administer in the ordinances of the Church.

All will agree that the Church of Jesus Christ of Latter Day Saints teaches all of the above. If a person does not teach all the above, then according to Paul, they are lying in wait to deceive and we can recognize them as a false teacher and certainly a false prophet.

CHAPTER 18

The Power of Prophecy

In studying the New Testament, I was astounded by the power of prophecies that had been uttered hundreds of years before and their binding power on the heavens to see to their fulfillment. This will deal with that subject. It reminds me of the words of Christ in D&C 1:37-38 where He says, "Search these commandments, for they are true and faithful, <u>and the prophecies and promises which are in them shall all be fulfilled.</u> What I the Lord have spoken, I have spoken, and I excuse not myself; and though the heavens and the earth pass away, my word shall not pass away, <u>but all shall be fulfilled, whether by mine own voice or the voice of my servants, it is the same.</u> Jesus says the same thing in 3 Nephi 15:6:"Behold, I do not destroy the prophets, for as many as have not been fulfilled in me, verily I say unto you, shall all be fulfilled."

So, let's study the prophecies regarding the life of Jesus and their fulfillment. Please note two things as we take this journey:

1. The power of the prophecy stated by mortal men called prophets;
2. The obedience of Heavenly Father and Jesus Christ to the fulfillment of the prophecy.

1. Isaiah 7:14 (2 Nephi 17:14) "Therefore the Lord himself shall give you a sign; Behold, a virgin shall conceive, and bear a son, and shall call his name Immanuel." <u>Fulfilled as stated in Matthew 1:21-25</u>. For how a virgin could conceive, see the paper THE CONDESCENSION OF GOD by Glenn R. Orr. Immanuel is a Hebrew word meaning God is with us. Jesus is the Greek word meaning "God is help" or Savior.

Look at the extent our Heavenly Father had to go to fulfill this prophecy! First, He had to send an angel to convince Mary that it was possible for a virgin to conceive. (Luke 1:26-35) The angel used as the final persuasive argument that Mary's cousin, Elizabeth-barren and well past child bearing age-was pregnant. Then once Mary was pregnant-of which she speaks almost in rapture in Luke 1:46-55-the angel had to convince Joseph to go ahead with the plans to wed Mary when he found out she was pregnant. See Matthew 1:19-25. Do you feel the binding power of prophecy?

2. Micah 5:2 "But thou, Bethlehem Ephratah, though thou be little among the thousands of Judah, yet out of thee shall he come forth unto me that is to be ruler in Israel; whose goings forth have been from of old, from everlasting." When restated to Herod, the wise men used the word, "Governor" instead of ruler.

   Talk about the binding power of prophecy! This one is a matter of timing. Think about this: Joseph and Mary lived in Nazareth of Galilee, about 100 miles from Bethlehem of Judea (or Judah). For this prophecy to be fulfilled, Joseph and Mary would have to have some reason to undertake the arduous many-day journey and her being <u>large in pregnancy</u>! For the first time in twenty years, Caesar Augustus ordered a "taxing" of all people in 1 B.C., which was an actual registration or an enrollment of the people. Respecting Jewish custom, they were required to register in their ancestral home which was the City of David or Bethlehem because they were both of the lineage of David. In addition, all in #1 above had to be timed so that this prophecy could be fulfilled! Just a coincidence? I don't think so! Elder Neal A. Maxwell of the Twelve Apostles calls it "micro-management" by our Heavenly Father. <u>The fulfillment of this prophecy is best told in Luke 2.</u>

3. Jeremiah 31:15 "Thus saith the Lord; A voice was heard in Rajah, lamentation, and bitter weeping; Rachel weeping for her children refused to be comforted for her children,

because they were not." This was fulfilled by Herod the Great (They called him "Great" because he built so many buildings. How about Herod the Murderer?) issuing his extermination order for children two years and younger in a vain attempt to kill the "Governor" as foretold in Micah 5:2 and repeated to Herod by his wise men as told in Matthew 1:6. Herod obviously had an awful case of paranoia to go to this extent to wipe out thousands in order to kill a possible competitor. <u>Yet he fulfilled prophecy in so doing when he issued the extermination order as stated in Matthew 2:16.</u>

4. In order to escape this terrible extermination order, an angel appeared to Joseph, instructing him to take Mary and Jesus to Egypt. Why Egypt? Why not escape to Arabia where Elizabeth took the infant John (later called John the Baptist)? It was to fulfill the prophecy of Hosea written in Hosea 11:1 "When Israel was a child, then I loved him, and called my son out of Egypt." <u>This is recounted in Mathew 2:13-15.</u> Heavenly Father sent an angel to tell Joseph to go to Egypt and then the angel told Joseph to return after the death of Herod The Murderer.

5. They returned to Nazareth rather than staying in Bethlehem to <u>fulfill prophecy as stated in Matthew 2:23</u> "And he came and dwelt in a city called Nazareth; that it might be fulfilled which was spoken by the prophets, He shall be called a Nazarene." <u>This prophecy is not found in the scriptures as we have them.</u> Lest you think they lived in the stables

until they went to Egypt, please note Matthew 1:11 where it says the wise men came to visit them in a "house" in Bethlehem. In addition, Herod's infant extermination order was for children two years old and younger. This leads one to believe that the visit of the wise men occurred a year or so after the birth of Jesus Christ and that Joseph and Mary had taken up residence in Bethlehem.

6. Approximately twenty years later Jesus starts His ministry. Where? It had been prophesied by Isaiah in 9:1-2. In Galilee. So Jesus went to Capernaum, on the northwest shore of the Sea of Galilee as told in Matthew 4:14 to fulfill the prophecy to start His ministry.

7. Isaiah 42:2 says, "He shall not cry, nor lift up, nor cause his voice to be heard in the street." Where did he preach and teach in a town or city? The usual place for a prophet was at the gate of the city or he would cry repentance to the people on the roads and streets. Obedient to prophecy, Jesus taught not in those places but on the seashore, on the mountainside and in the synagogues (Matthew 9:35). The prophecy is restated in Matthew 12:19. It could also be fulfilled in His conduct when brought before Pilate and his walk to Golgotha.

8. Why did Jesus heal the sick? To fulfill prophesy. In 1 Nephi 11:31 Nephi writes, "And he (he is the Spirit of the Lord-1 Nephi 11:11) spake unto me again, saying: Look! And I looked, and I beheld the Lamb of God going forth among

the children of men. And I beheld multitudes of people who were sick, and who were aflicted with all manner of diseases, and with devils and unclean spirits; and the angel spake and showed all these things unto me. And they were healed by the power of the Lamb of God; and the devils and the unclean spirits were cast out. <u>Fulfilled as stated in numerous places in Matthew such as 4:23</u>

9. Why did Jesus speak in parables? To fulfill prophecy and it was prophesied by Isaiah in 6:9 (2 Nephi 16:9-10) says, addressing the people "...Go, and tell this people, "Hear ye indeed, but understand not; and see ye indeed, but perceive not. (10) Make the heart of this people fat, and make their ears heavy, and shut their eyes; lest they see with their eyes, and hear with their cars, and understand with their heart, and convert, and be healed." (The quotations are added because this is what the Lord commanded Isaiah to say and write.) The disciples asked Jesus also why he spake in parables as quoted in Matthew 13:10 and <u>He answered them as quoted in Matthew 13:13 that it was to be obedient to the prophecy of Isaiah as quoted above</u>. In Luke 8:10 He tells His disciples (converts) that He will explain the meaning to them but to the people He will talk in parables. The reason is that the people are too close-minded and neither will believe what they hear nor what they see! That is why Jesus said in the Sermon on the Mount, "Give not that which is holy unto the dogs, neither cast ye your pearls before swine,...

10. The prophet, Zechariah, prophesied, "Rejoice,...thy King cometh unto thee: he is just and having salvation; lowly, riding upon an ass, and upon the colt of a foal of an ass." (Zechariah 9:8) <u>This was fulfilled exactly in Matthew 21:1-7.</u>

11. Jesus explains vividly in Matthew 26:53 that He could stop all these events which were leading to crucifixion. "Thinkest thou thatI cannot now pray to my Father, and he shall presently give me more than twelve legions of angels?" He also explains why he doesn't: "But how then shall the scriptures be fulfilled that thus it must be?" (Matthew 26:53-54)

12. One of the great mysteries is this: How could a people or a group of people, who had seen a man perform miracles in healing and the casting out of devils, had seen him bring back the dead to living, had seen him do no wrong (except in the eyes of the Sanhedrin-heal on the Sabbath and cast the money changers out of the temple twice), had even seen him heal the ear of the servant of Caiaphas, the high priest when Peter cut if off, how could they cause that he should be crucified-the most excruciatingly painful method of death known? How could they do that? He had preached peace, forgiving 70 times seven, turning the other cheek. How could they crucify this lamb? The answer is somewhat complex and is described in WHY DIDN'T THE JEWS RECOGNIZE CHRIST? by Glenn R. Orr. To condense it, the Jews were expecting a King-Messiah (second coming)

rather than a Messiah (first coming). They wanted the grandeur of David's kingdom returned rather than a restoration of the Church and the Gospel in its fullness. In addition, the plan of salvation of man was involved. Again, it was also to fulfill the prophecy of Isaiah (6:9-10) who said on behalf of the Lord, "And he said, Go, and tell this people, Hear ye indeed, but understand not. Make the heart of this people fat (hardened), and make their ears heavy, shut their eyes; lest they see with their eyes, and hear with their ears, and understand with their heart, and convert, and be healed. (spiritually)" Then in John 12:40, Isaiah is quoted a little differently but with the same meaning: "He hath blinded their eyes, and hardened their heart; that they should not see with their eyes, nor understand with their heart; and be converted, and I should heal them."

13. Who would be the informer? Several times Jesus had been in situations where they wanted to take him and he would disappear. So, who would betray him? Surely, not one of the Apostles! Who? The Psalmist prophesied in Psalms 41:9 "Yea, mine own familiar friend, in whom I trusted, which did eat of my bread, hath lifted up his heel against me." It is one of the Apostles! Jesus is quoted in John 13:18 as saying this exact thing: "...but that the scripture may be fulfilled, He that eateth bread with me hath lifted up his heel against me." It was the bagman Apostle (the keeper of their money), Judas Iscariot. This was also to fulfill prophecy as Jesus gave his great intercessory prayer in John 17. He

prayed to his Heavenly Father and in the prayer he said, "...those thou gavest me I have kept, and none of them is lost, but the son of perdition; (Judas) that the scripture might be fulfilled." What scripture? I can't find it. But Jesus knew it!

14. Matthew 27:9 says that Jeremy or Jeremiah had prophesied regarding the purchase of the potter's field with the 30 pieces of silver that Judas Iscariot had returned to the chief priests after he had betrayed Jesus Christ and been paid for the betrayal. We have no record of it in the Book of Jeremiah which shows we do not have all of Jeremiah's prophecies but in the Book of Zechariah, 11:12-13 it talks about it briefly. Also, 30 pieces of silver was the price for a slave.

15. Jesus could easily have confounded his accusers by several methods but he by-in-large kept silent or the plan for his crucifixion and resurrection would have failed. This too, was prophesied by Isaiah in 42:2 where he says, "He shall not cry, nor lift up, nor cause his voice to be heard in the street."

16. Isaiah 53:12 says, "..and he was numbered with the transgressors; and he bare the sin of many, and made intercession for the transgressors. This could refer to several times in Jesus' life for he left the ninety and nine on several occasions to heal the one. However, it is quoted in Mark 15:28 to apply to the time on the cross when he was with the two thieves.

17. David, speaking messianically says in Psalms 22:18, "They part my garments among them, and cast lots upon my vesture." This was fulfilled in Matthew 27:35 (Mark 15:24, Luke 23:34, John 19:24) Vesture was the outer garment or coat and John "They part my garments among them, and cast lots upon my vesture." describes it best in 19:23-24: Then the soldiers, when they had crucified Jesus, took his garments, and made four parts, to every soldier a part; (obviously there were four soldiers) and also his coat; now the coat was without seam, woven from the top through- out. They said therefore among themselves, Let us not rend it (tear it up) but cast lots for it, whose it shall be; that the scripture might be fulfilled, (Even the soldiers knew of the prophecy??) which saith, They parted my raiment among them and for my vesture they did cast lots. These things therefore the soldiers did."

18. David, again speaking messianically, foretells in Psalm 22:1: "My God, my God, why hast thou forsaken me? This is fulfilled in Matthew 27:46: And about the ninth hour Jesus cried with a loud voice, saying, Eli, Eli, lama sabachthani? that is to say, My God, my God, why hast thou forsaken me.?" This is stated more correctly in Mark 15:34 where it uses Eloi rather than Eli. Eloi would be the singular of Elohim, God of Gods.

19. It was now shortly before sunset and Jesus had been on the cross since 9 a.m. according to Mark 15:25 and since noon

according to John 19:14-16. (See Contradictions, #4 by Glenn R. Or for more details) Sunset in April in Jerusalem would be approximately 7:30 p.m. so he had been hanging on the cross for many hours. However, this kind of death was very slow and very painful. With the Sabbath approaching, the Jews asked that the legs of all three be broken to end their life so that they would not break the Sabbath by being on the cross on the Sabbath! (The breaking of the legs would not allow them to stand and take the pressure off their arms so they could breath. So death would be by asphyxiation. Is that the letter of the law rather than the spirit or what?? (John 19:31) However, there was one prophecy yet Jesus had to fulfill which would allow two other prophecies to be fulfilled after his death. 1. One is found in Psalms 69:21: "... and in my thirst they gave me vinegar to drink." This was fulfilled in John 19:28: "After this, Jesus, knowing that all things were now accomplished, (all prophecies had been fulfilled except one) that the scripture might be fulfilled, saith I thirst." Then they gave him vinegar. 2. For him to fulfill the next prophecy Jesus had to die quickly before sunset which he did (verse 30) "...and he bowed his head, and gave up the ghost." Understand, he gave up his life and I am convinced he did it to fulfill these last two prophecies: "He keepeth all his bones; not one of them is broken." (Psalms 34:20. <u>This was fulfilled in John 19:32-36:</u> "Then came the soldiers, and brake the legs of the first, and of the other which was crucified with him. But when they came to Jesus, and saw that he was dead already, they brake not his legs:" In John 19:35, John bears his testimony that he saw it all. 3. The final prophecy fulfilled in the crucifixion is found in Zechariah 12:10: "..and they shall look upon me whom they have <u>pierced,</u> and they shall mourn for him,..." <u>This is fulfilled in John 19:34:</u> "But one of the soldiers with a spear pierced his side, and forthwith came there out blood and water.

20. Then after Jesus' resurrection He told the Apostles in Luke 24:44: "..These are the words which I spake unto you, while I was yet with you, that <u>all things must be fulfilled, which were written in the law of Moses, and in the prophets, and in the psalms, concerning me."</u>

We hope that as a result of reading this paper, three conclusions will become apparent to you:

1. Heavenly Father and Jesus Christ are obedient to the words of their prophets. Therefore, we must do the same.

2. We are so fortunate to have guiding us a living prophet. We must listen to our prophet's voice and do as he counsels.

3. We cannot be "lukewarm" in following their counsel, picking and choosing that which we will obey. John says in Revelations 3:16: "So then because thou are lukewarm and neither cold nor hot, I will spue thee out of my mouth."

We need to adopt the enthusiastic attitude of Peter in John 13. Jesus was anointing the feet of the Apostles and Peter didn't want Jesus to do such a menial task. Jesus said, "If I wash thee not, thou hast no part of me." Peter responded enthusiastically, "Lord, not my feet only, but also my hands and my head." (John 13:9) That is the way we need to immerse ourselves in the work! All the way!!!

CHAPTER 19

Prophecies of Joseph Smith, Jr

NOTE: There are literally hundreds of Joseph's prophecies, forewarnings, foreknowledge, etc., that he gave that have been fulfilled. These pages are but a sample. The way to tell if a person is a prophet is simple, his prophecies come true! Let's see:

<u>**PROPHECY (Date given in bold type)**</u>　　Fulfilled
　　　　　　　　　　　　　　　　　　　　(Date fulfilled)

1. The fullness of the gospel shall at some future time be made known unto me. **(April, 1820)** Fulfilled by the translation of the Book of Mormon and the restoration of the gospel and the fullness. (1827-1843)

2. The angel said the Lord will send me a scribe. **(September 22, 1828)**. Fulfilled by the arrival of Oliver

Cowdery who was the primary scribe, save a few pages, for the entire Book of Mormon. (April 3, 1829)

3. **Martin Harris shall say nothing concerning the plates except that he has seen them by the power of God. (March, 1829)** Martin Harris, later excommunicated December, 1837, rebaptized September 17, 1870, and died July 10, 1875, never denied seeing the plates. "My disbelief is swallowed up in my knowledge that I did see the Angel who showed us the golden plates.in the brightness of the day" (1875)

4. **Joseph knew of David Whitmer's work being expedited by angels so that he could come for Oliver, Joseph and Emma to take them to Fayette, New York. (early June, 1829)** Joseph told Oliver about the Angels helping David expedite his farm work, so his father, Peter Witmer, would allow David to leave and Joseph foresaw his arrival time. A beautiful story.

5. **(To Newel K Whitney) You prayed me here, now what do you want of me? (February 1, 1831)** Joseph had seen in a vision the Whitneys praying when he was 200 miles from them. The Whitney's had been praying to receive the Holy Ghost and in a vision heard a voice saying, "Prepare to receive the word of the Lord, for it is coming" . It came!

6. **I will someday shelter the Whitneys in my home. (1831)** When Joseph and Emma first arrived in Kirtland

they stayed at the Whitney's, a very prosperous merchant. It was inconceivable that the prophecy would ever come true but it did as the Whitney's stayed with Joseph and Emma at Nauvoo until they could get on their own again (1840)

7. **(To Newel K Whitney) if you will start for home in the morning, take a wagon to the river, there will be a ferryboat to take you across where you will find a hack to take you directly to the landing where there will be a boat waiting. We will be going up the river before 10 o'clock and have a prosperous journey home. (June, 1832)** Bro Whitney had been injured and was returning to Kirtland from Missouri with Joseph. After the above foretelling, they immediately left and found all the conveyances as foretold!

8. **The Bishopric shall never be taken away from Newel K Whitney while he liveth. (December 4, 1831)** Fulfilled as he was the Bishop of Kirtland, then of Nauvoo, then Presiding Bishop first in Winter Quarters and then in Salt Lake City until his death on September 23, 1850!

9. **The time will come when Brigham Young will preside over this church. (September, 1832)** Fulfilled in 1844 and named second President December 5, 1847 and presided until his death, August 9, 1877

10. **Wars are nigh, even at your doors, and not many years hence you shall hear of wars in your own lands. (March 7, 1831)** Fulfilled in the Civil War, Starting in 1861

11. **Wars will begin with the rebellion of South Carolina. (December 25, 1832)** Fulfilled 29 years later when the rebellion started by the firing on the Union troops at Fort Sumter, South Carolina. (April 12, 1861) According to books I have read, the divisive sentiment between the North and the South in the 1830's was not over the slavery issue but cotton and the selling to France by the South.

12. **(To skeptics in Kirtland about Joseph being a prophet) Forty days shall not pass and the stars shall fall from heaven. (Fall of 1833)** Fulfilled 39 days later when the falling stars and meteors lit up the whole sky and were visible all over the whole United States. (4 AM, November 13, 1833) Many of the skeptics joined the Church after that!

13. **In a short time the Lord will send us deliverance from debt. (1834 while so very poor and yet obeying the commandment to build the temple)** It was fulfilled by the members' commitment to sacrifice money-which they had little of-and their time. (1836)

14. **Kirtland Safety Society notes will one day be as good as gold. (1836)** This bank collapsed, causing charges of

"fallen prophet" and apostasy by some leaders even after being forewarned by Joseph. Prophecy was fulfilled in Utah when it was used as currency and put on par with gold because they had no other currency. (1847)

15. **A sermon will be preached in Jackson County before the close of 1838. (Summer of 1838)** Remember, Saints had been run out of Jackson County in 1833 and Gov. Boggs' extermination order was issued October 27, 1838 so likelihood of fulfillment was almost nil. However, while Joseph was a prisoner in Independence Missouri-Jackson County-several well-to-do men and women came to see him and he preached to them on the gospel at their request. The people-nonmembers-went away, praying for his protection and deliverance. (November 4, 1838)

16. **In the great cities, such as Boston, New York City, etc., there will be stakes. (1844-Nauvoo)** Fulfilled in Boston May 20, 1962 and fulfilled in New York December 9, 1934.

17. **(To General Doniphan) I advise you not to take Jackson County land in payment of debt, for God's wrath hangs over Jackson County. The fields and farms and houses-in Jackson County-will be destroyed, and only the chimneys will be left to mark the desolation. (1838)** This was fulfilled in the Civil War when the Union Army issued Order Number 11 which

ordered the citizens of Jackson, Cass and Bates counties to evacuate so they could wipe out the Southerners. They didn't so they burned the houses, killed the livestock, molested the citizens-like they had done to the Mormons in July, 1833-. Fulfilled in 1864.

18. **President of the United States-Martin Van Buren will never be elected again to any office of trust or power by which he may abuse the innocent and let the guilty go free. (March 4, 1840)** Stated after Joseph returned from seeking redress from the Missouri sufferings. Martin Van Buren was president from 1837-1841. He was defeated in 1840, 1844 and 1848 for the office of president. He died in 1862, never having been elected to another office!

19. **I prophesied to Judge Stephen A Douglas, then a circuit judge in Illinois. "Judge, you will aspire to the presidency of the United States. If you ever turn your hand against me or the Latter Day Saints, you will feel the weight of the hand of the Almighty and you will remember this day." (1841)** In the 1860 election Stephen A Douglas, the great orator, was highly favored over Abraham Lincoln and two other candidates. In order to win votes he turned against the Mormons. He received the smallest number of votes of the four candidates! {1860)He died less than a year later, a very disappointed and brokenhearted man.

20. **I will not live to see 40 years.(1842)** He was murdered at age 38 (June 27, 1844)

21. **The Saints will continue to suffer much afflictions. They will be driven to the Rocky Mountains. Many will apostatize. Many will be put to death by our persecutors or lose their lives in consequence of exposure or disease. Some of you will go and assist in making settlements and build cities and see the Saints become a mighty people in the Rocky Mountains. (August 6, 1842)** The Saints never left until 1846 but certainly this prophecy has come to pass.

22. **(To Willard Richards) the time will come that the balls (musket balls) will fly around you like hail, and you shall see your friends fall on the right and on the left, but there shall not be one hole in your garment. (1843)** Willard Richards was with Joseph, Hyrum and John Taylor at the Carthage Jail. Joseph and Hyrum were killed and John was shot five times-one of which was stopped by his pocket watch-and barely escaped death. With the hail of bullets and musket balls from the mob and the large size of Willard Richards-over 300 pounds-it was miraculous that none hit him but the prophecy was fulfilled. (June 27, 1844)

23. **I prophesy that I shall not go to Missouri dead or alive. (January 2, 1843)** He never did, in spite of all the arrests-42 In 1843 alone-and kidnapping attempts.

24. **As soon as we get the Temple built, we will have means to gather the saints by the thousands and tens of thousands. (January 20, 1843)** This was referring to Nauvoo. It became a city of 20,000, largest in Illinois before they were driven out.

25. **(To the Nauvoo Police) Not one of you shall ever be harmed for what you have done (destroying the Nauvoo Expositor) . (June 7, 1844)** Later, after the martyrdom of Joseph and Hyrum-June 27, 1844, three of the police were tried and acquitted.

26. **My son Joseph will be the means of drawing many people away from this Church after him. (June 1, 1844)** Fulfilled 16 years later. At first, Joseph III refused them, but after having failed in other occupations, he allowed himself to be elected as President of the Reorganized Church (April 6, 1860)

27. **Sickness will enter into the houses of the mob and vex them until they repent. They will be smitten with the scab. Their flesh will be meat for wolves. (June 6, 1844)** Whole books have been written on the fate of the persecutors, none of it good. Several had wounds that kept rotting until they died. Some contracted cholera and died on the plains on the way to the gold strike .(1849) "wolves eating their flesh". There are many other terrible occurrences in fulfillment of this prophecy.

28. If I and Hyrum are ever taken again we shall be massacred, or I am not a prophet of God. (June 22, 1844)
Joseph and Hyrum were arrested two days later and massacred five days later. The prophecy was fulfilled.

Aren't these amazing? These should be enough to convince the sharpest critic that Joseph is a true prophet of God just as surely as were Moses, Jeremiah, Isaiah, Lehi, Nephi, Moroni and others.

CHAPTER 20

Tests to Show Mormons Are a Cult

(As proposed in the book, "New Cults" by Walter Martin)

"New Cults" definition of a Cult:

1. Strong Leaders-Yes, we have them.
2. The claim to additional scriptures-Absolutely!
3. Maintaining rigid standards for members-The only way.
4. Membership consisting largely of converts-How else??
5. Active proselytizing-Yes!
6. Having no professional clergy-same way with the New Testament Church as taught by Paul and Peter.
7. Being in a state of flux i.e., Having no fixed creed. Wonderful, we can change with the times as did Jesus.

8. A belief in continual revelation-absolutely, if we believe in a living God who speaks through his prophets.

9. The exclusive claim to possession of the truths of salvation-yes, guilty again as specified by Jesus.

10. Possession of a cultic vocabulary-thee, thou, thy and thine could be called cultic.

Yes, we're guilty. We are a cult, as defined above by the Anti's. But wait a minute, we are in great company! Besides us having all of the above characteristics, look at Jesus Christ, his disciples and the Early Church. It has all the same characteristics!! By the way, have you ever heard of a "cult" having over 16,000,000 members?

CHAPTER 21

Why Do You Say on the Cover, "Skeptical and Scriptural" in Your Review?

Because of my experience in other religious organizations.

While I was a member of the Southern Baptist Church, they ranted and shouted (Don't Baptist preachers always shout?) before the offering plates were passed every Sunday. I have heard that they would pass the plates around again if the plates were not filled. All about money.

While I was in practice in Iowa I attended the Lutheran Church as most of my clients were good German Lutherans. A few months after starting my practice, one of my clients, a Lutheran elder on their board, stopped me and said he needed to talk to me. I assumed it was about one of his livestock. Instead, he said. "Dr Orr, you need to quit giving so much to the church." I said, "Alvie, that is between me and the Lord". I forgot he was one of the elders. He was drunk every Saturday night but was in church every Sunday like many of those good Germans. He then told me the real reason. "It might be embarrassing to some when the results are published in January." I was shocked. Everybody will see what everybody gave?? I thought about it and said, "Alvie, if my name is published that I gave one penny, I will never pay my tithe to your church again." He said he would see what he could do. In January, guess what, my name was not published and wasn't for the next eight years.. I looked at it and I had given more than Alvie or any of my rich clients who sure made much more than I did. Obviously, they gave to impress one another, sort of like a competition. What about the 6th chapter of Matthew verses 2-6 where Jesus says we should pray and tithe in secret?

Then in another business of mine, I dealt with eight Bible broadcasters who had been given 1/8th of 1/3rd of the net income by the former land holder, Connie Chase of Chevy Chase Apartments. The problem was there was no net income and we were barely able to pay all the bills and we were getting nothing for managing them. I called them Barracudas as these representatives-usually 2 for each ⅛-would smile at our semi-annual meeting and then try to eat me alive. They tried to break my 99 year lease and lost. All about the money. Later the apartments started making money and I

Why Do You Say on the Cover, "Skeptical and Scriptural"

sold them to a California REIT and took back a second with the proviso that they must first buy out the Barracudas. The reason for that was that if I had to take them back I wouldn't have to deal with them any longer. Oklahoma City got overbuilt again and I had to foreclose so this time we owned them outright.

So, I was skeptical when I joined the Church of Jesus Christ of Latter Day Saints that I would see that money was the main concern of the leaders. The first thing I noticed was that there was no collection plate passed. While we were attending and before I joined I don't recall any mention of tithing in the Sunday meetings. After I was baptized and six weeks of not paying tithing, I was puzzled and asked the bishop how I was to pay my tithing and he told me. Turns out that about every six to eight weeks someone is asked to speak on tithing. I never saw anything like I had experienced before and years later when I dealt with the First Presidency and the Twelve Apostles in one of my callings and even at that level it was never brought up. Whew! What a relief!. Yet, I have seen it published that we are the highest percentage tithe payers in the world. Obviously, it is not necessary to talk about-or shout about-tithing all the time. We put money or a check in an envelope and hand it to the Bishop or one of his counselors usually after a payday. Very private. The Book of Mormon says it even clearer in 3 Nephi 13:1 "...but take heed that ye do not your alms before men to be seen of them; otherwise ye have no reward in heaven." (you can't be rewarded twice!) And in verse four "That thine alms may be in secret; and thy Father who seeth in secret, himself shall reward thee openly"

CHAPTER 22

Contradictions in the New Testament

Note: In the 8th Article of Faith, Joseph Smith stated, "We believe the Bible to be the word of God as far as it is translated correctly;" This chapter is for those who believe that there are no mistranslations in the Bible, that every word must be believed "as it is" or one does not believe in the Bible. Boy, after reading the following, those people are going to be really confused!

1. <u>Matthew 1:18,20 contradicts Luke 1:31,35</u>

    a. Matthew 1:18 says, "Now the birth of Jesus Christ was on this wise: When as his mother Mary was espoused to Joseph, before they came together, she was found with child of the Holy Ghost. 20 "...for that which is conceived in her is of the Holy Ghost." This indicates that the Holy Ghost is the father of Jesus Christ.

123

b. Luke 1:34-35 (When the angel was telling Mary that she would conceive the Son of the Highest) says, "Then said Mary unto the angel, How shall this be, seeing I know not a man? 35. And the angel answered and said unto her, The Holy Ghost shall come upon thee, and the **power of the Highest (God) shall overshadow thee; therefore also that holy thing which shall be born of thee shall be called the Son of God."** This indicates that God is the father of Jesus, not the Holy Ghost.

CONTRADICTION: One says Jesus Christ is the son of God while the other says Jesus is the son of the Holy Ghost.

SOLUTION: 1 Nephi 11:16-21 says, "And he said unto me: Knowest thou the condescension of God? 17. And I said unto him: I know that he loveth his children; nevertheless, I do not know the meaning of all things. 18. And he said unto me: Behold, the virgin whom thou seest is the mother of the Son of God, after the manner of the flesh. 19. And it came to pass that I beheld that she was carried away in the Spirit; and after she had been carried away in the Spirit for the space of a time the angel spake unto me, saying: Look! 20. And I looked and beheld the virgin again, bearing a child in her arms. 21. And the angel said unto me: Behold the Lamb of God, yea, even the Son of the Eternal Father!" Remember, we are all the spirit children of our Heavenly Father. However, this explains why and how Jesus bears the name, The Only Begotten of the Father!

2. Matthew 1:16 contradicts Luke 3:23

    a. Matthew 1:16 says the father of Joseph was Jacob
    b. Luke 3:23 says the father of Joseph was Heli

CONTRADICTION: One says that Joseph, the husband of Mary who was the mother of Jesus, was Jacob and the other Heli.

SOLUTION: Joseph and Mary were cousins. Jacob and Heli were brothers. It is felt by Bible scholars that Matthew's account is the Davidic lineage to fulfill prophecy (Gen 12:3; Ps. 132; Isa. 11: Jer. 23:5; Gal. 3:16, D&C 113:1) to convince the Jews of the lineage of Joseph. Luke's description also goes back to David but many feel it is the lineage of Mary. So, one brother is the father of Joseph and the other brother is the father of Mary! (DNTC p. 92-95) It is still a contradiction.

3. Matthew 9:18 contradicts Mark 5:23 and Luke 8:42

    a. Matthew 9:18 says, "...My daughter is even now dead."
    b. Mark 5:23 says, "..My little daughter lieth at the point of death:"
    c. Luke 8:41 says, "..For he had one (JST corrected to an) only daughter, about twelve years of age, and she lay a dying."

CONTRADICTION: One says Jairus' daughter is dead while the other two say she is dying.

SOLUTION: Joseph Smith corrected Matthew 9:18 to read dying instead of dead. This is talking about Jairus, ruler of the synagogue at Capernaum, seeking Jesus to save the life of his only daughter. By the time they arrived at Jairus" home she had died. Jesus removed all the mourners and healed her.

4. Mark 15:25 contradicts John 19:14-16

   a. Mark 15:25 says, "And it was the third hour, (9 am) and they crucified him."

   b. John 19:14-16 says, "And it was the preparation of the passover, and about the sixth hour (noon): and he (Pontius Pilate) saith unto the Jews, Behold your King! But they cried out, Away with him, away with him, crucify him. Pilate saith unto them, Shall I crucify your King? The chief priests answered, We have no king but Caesar. Then delivered he him therefore unto them to be crucified. And they took Jesus, and led him away."

CONTRADICTION: Was it noon or 9 am when Jesus was crucified?

SOLUTION: Elder James E. Talmage in Jesus the Christ says they probably nailed him to the cross between 9 am and 10 am. (Jesus the Christ, page 660). Skousen says that they probably crucified Jesus at noon (the sixth hour) because of all the activities of the morning. (Days of the Living Christ, Volume I, page 735. Therefore, there is still confusion!

5. <u>Matthew 27:46 contradicts Mark 15:34</u>

   a. Matthew 27:46 says, "Eli, Eli, lama sabachthani? that is to say, My God, My God, why hast thou forsaken me?* Verse 46 says, "Some of them that stood there, when they heard that, said, This man calleth for Elias." <u>Eli means exalted one</u>.

   b. Mark 15:34 says, "Eloi, Eloi, lama sabachthani? which is, being interpreted, My God, My God, why hast thou forsaken me?" Verse 35 says, "And some of them that stood by, when they heard it, said, Behold, he calleth Elias."

CONTRADICTION: One says Jesus cried for Eli and the other Eloi.

SOLUTION: Without a doubt, Jesus called for Eloi, the singular and the personal (familiar-held for loved ones) of Elohim, (meaning God of Gods) his father.

6. <u>John 1:18, 1 Timothy 6:16, 1 John 4:12 and others contradict Matthew 5:8, Matthew 11:27, John 6:46, John 14:21, Acts 7:56, Hebrews 12:14, 1 John 3:2, 3 John 1:11 and Revelations 22:4.</u>

Are the Mormons Teaching Fables

1. **SCRIPTURES IN THE OLD TESTAMENT THAT STATE THAT NO MAN HAS SEEN GOD:**

   a. In Exodus 33:20 the Lord says to Moses, "...Thou canst not see my face; for there shall no man see me, and live."

2. **SCRIPTURES IN THE NEW TESTAMENT THAT STATE NO MAN HAS SEEN GOD:**

   a. John 1:18 says, "No man hath seen God at any time; the only begotten Son, which is in the bosom of the Father, he hath declared him."

   b. 1 Timothy 6:16 says, "Who (Paul is talking about Jesus Christ) only hath immortality, dwelling in the light which no man can approach unto; whom no man hath seen, nor can see: to whom be honour and power everlasting. Amen." How could Paul say this when Paul had seen the glory of Jesus Christ on the road to Damascus and been blinded by it??

   c. 1 John 4:12 says, "No man hath seen God at any time. If we love one another, God dwelleth in us, and his love is perfected in us."

3. **SCRIPTURES IN THE OLD TESTAMENT THAT STATE THAT MAN SAW GOD**

   a. Genesis 32:30 Jacob says, "...I have seen God face to face, and my life is preserved."

CONTRADICTIONS IN THE NEW TESTAMENT

   b. Exodus 24:9-10 says that seventy-four men saw the God of Israel!

   c. Exodus 33:11 says, "And the Lord spake unto Moses face to face, as a man speaketh unto his friend."

   d. Deuteronomy 34:10 says, "...Moses, whom the Lord knew face to face."

   e. 1 Kings 11:9 the God of Israel had appeared unto Solomon twice.

   f. Isaiah 6:1 & 5 says that Isaiah saw the King of Israel, meaning the God of Israel.

4. SCRIPTURES IN THE NEW TESTAMENT THAT STATE MAN MAY SEE GOD BY DOING CERTAIN THINGS:

   a. Matthew 5:8 says, "Blessed are the pure in heart; for they shall see God." Jesus says this.

   b. Matthew 11:27 is exactly in line with Joseph's clarification of John 1:18 when it says, "All things are delivered unto me of my Father; and no man knoweth the Son, but the Father;, neither knoweth any man the Father, save the Son, and he to whomsoever the Son will reveal him."

   c. John 6:46 contradicts what he says in John 1:18 and 1 John 4:12 when he says, "Not that any man hath seen the Father, save he which is of God, he hath seen the Father."

d. John 14:21 (the same writer as 2 a. & 2 b. above) says, "He that hath my commandments, and keepeth them, he it is that loveth me; and he that loveth me shall be loved of my Father, and I will love him, and will manifest (show) myself to him." Jesus was here talking about after he was resurrected. Manifest means to show or see.

e. Acts 7:56 Luke writes what Stephen says about Stephen's vision, "Behold, I see the heavens opened, and the Son of man standing on the right hand of God." **He saw God and Jesus Christ**.

f. Hebrews 12:14 Paul says, "Follow peace with all men, and holiness, without which no man shall see the Lord:"

g. 1 John 3:2 John (the same writer of a. & b. above) says, "Beloved, now are the sons (children) of God, and it doth not yet appear what we shall be; but we know that, when he shall appear, we shall be like him; for we shall see him as he is." Obviously, John had seen God. Otherwise he couldn't make such a statement.

h. 3 John 1:11 The same writer as above says, "Beloved, follow not that which is evil, but that which is good. He that doeth good is of God; but he that doeth evil hath not seen God." From that statement it is logical to assume that those who do good can see God, as stated in Matthew 5:8 and John 14:21.

i. Revelations 22:4 speaking after the milleanium, "And they shall see his (God's) face; and his (God's) name shall be on their foreheads.

CONTRADICTION: Can we see God or not? No wonder there was such confusion over God, whether he is a personage as we are-as it says in Genesis 1:26-27-or whether he is an "essence" as declared in the Nicene Council in 325 AD by approximately 318 of the leading Bishops in the Universal (Catholic) Church. If God is a "mist" or "essence", does that make Jesus Christ, his Only Begotten a mist and us little mists??

SOLUTION:

a. Joseph corrects the contradiction in Exodus 33:20, "And he said unto Moses, Thou canst not see my face at this time, lest mine anger be kindled against thee also, and I destroy thee, and thy people; for there shall no man among them see me at this time, and live, for they are exceedingly sinful. And no sinful man hath at any time, neither shall there be any sinful man at any time, that shall see my face and live." That makes sense!

b. Joseph corrects John 1:18 to read, "No man hath seen God at any time except he hath borne record of the Son: for except it is through him (the Son) no man can be saved." Elder Bruce R. McConkie calls the King James Version of John 1:18 "..one of the classical examples of mistranslation.

c. Joseph corrects 1 John 4:12 to read, "No man hath seen God at any time, <u>except them who believe</u>."

d. Joseph Smith clarified 1 Timothy 6:16 to read, "Whom no man hath seen, nor can see, unto whom no man can approach, only he who hath the light and the hope of immortality dwelling in him."

e. D&C S8:3 explains a great deal when it says, "Ye cannot behold with your natural eyes, for the present time, the design of your God concerning those things which shall come hereafter, and the glory..."

f. D&C 67:11 says, "For no man has seen God at any time in the flesh, except quickened by the Spirit of God."

g. D&C 84:22 says, "without this (the Holy Ghost) no man can see the face of God...and live" In verse 23 it continues, "Now this Moses plainly taught to the children of Israel in the wilderness, and sought diligently to sanctify his people that they might behold the face of God."

7. <u>John 4:2 contradicts John 3:22 and John 3:26</u>

a. John 3:22 says, "After these things came Jesus and his disciples into the land of Judea; and there he tarried with them, and baptized.

b. John 3:26 says, "And they came unto John, and said unto him, Rabbi, he that was with thee beyond Jordan, to whom thou barest witness, behold, the same baptizeth and all men come to him.

c. John 4:2 says, "(Though Jesus himself baptized not, but his disciples,)"

CONTRADICTION: John 4:2 says Jesus never baptized anyone but the other two say he baptized.

SOLUTION: Joseph Smith clarified John 4:2: "..though he himself baptized not so many as his disciples; For he suffered them for an example, preferring one another."

8. John 4:2 contradicts Matthew 3:11, Mark 1:7-8 and Luke 3:16

   a. Matthew 3:11 says, "I (John the Baptist) indeed baptize you with water unto repentance: but he that cometh after me is mightier than I, whose shoes I am not worthy to bear: he shall baptize you with the Holy Ghost, and with fire:"

   b. Mark 1:7-8 says, "And preached, (John the Baptist) saying, There cometh one mightier than I after me, the latchet of whose shoes I am not worth to stoop down and unloose. I indeed have baptized you with water; but he shall baptize you with the Holy Ghost."

   c. Luke 3:16 says, "John answered, saying unto them all, I indeed baptize you with water; but one mightier than I cometh, the latchet of whose shoes I am not worthy to unloose; he shall baptize you with the Holy Ghost and with fire;"

d. John 4:2 says, "(Though Jesus himself baptized not, but his disciples,)"

CONTRADICTION: JOHN 4:2 MAKES JOHN THE BAPTIST A FALSE PROPHET!

SOLUTION: Joseph Smith clarified John 4:2: "...though he himself baptized not so many as his disciples; For he suffered them for an example, preferring one another."

9. <u>Matthew 27:5 contradicts Acts 1:18</u>

   a. Matthew 27:5 says Judas "...hanged himself."
   b. Acts 1:18 says Judas ".and falling headlong, he burst asunder in the midst, and all his bowels gushed out."

CONTRADICTION: Did Judas hang himself or fall on something that ruptured his stomach?

SOLUTION: Joseph removes the contradiction by changing. the wording of Matthew 27:5 to read, "...and hanged himself on a tree. And straightway he fell down, and his bowels gushed out, and he died." He did both! Judas couldn't even hang himself successfully. Disemboweling is second only to crucifixion in the agony it causes. Possibly we should feel compassion for Judas?

10. <u>Matthew 27:9-10 says the prophecy was made by Jeremy (Jeremiah) but it is found in the Bible in Zechariah 11:13</u>

CONTRADICTION: Is the prophecy found in Jeremiah or Zechariah?

SOLUTION: Probably the same prophecy was made by Jeremiah and left out and Zechariah repeated it.

11. <u>Matthew 28:2-7 and Mark 16:5-7l are contradicted by Luke 24:2-4</u>

    a. Matthew 28:2-7 and Mark 16:5-7 say there was one angel
    b. Luke 24:2-4 says there were two angels

CONTRADICTION: Which was it, one or two angels? Not important? It is still a contradiction.

SOLUTION: Joseph solved it by changing Matthew 28:2 to read ..."<u>two angels</u>" and verse 3 to read, "And <u>their</u> countenance was like lightning, and their raiment white as snow."

12. <u>Acts 9:7 contradicts Acts 22:9, both written by Luke.</u>

    a. Acts 9:7 says, "And the men which journeyed with him stood speechless, <u>hearing a voice</u>, but seeing no man.
    b. Acts 22:9 says, "And they that were with me saw indeed the light, and were afraid; but they <u>heard not the voice</u> of him that spake to me."

CONTRADICTION: One says the men who were with Paul heard a voice but did not see the light. The other says they saw the light but heard not the voice.

SOLUTION: Joseph Smith corrected Acts 9:7: "And they who were journeying with him saw indeed the light, and were afraid; but they heard not the voice of him (Jesus) who spake to him. (Paul)"

13. <u>1 Corinthians 10:24 contradicts about everything in the scriptures including the commandment-Thou shalt not steal.</u>

    a. 1 Corinthians 10:24 says, "Let no man seek his own, but every man another's wealth."

CONTRADICTION: We should seek (steal) another man's wealth?

SOLUTION: Joseph Smith corrected it to "..another's good." So simple, meaning his welfare. Now it is in harmony with the rest of the scriptures.

14. Galatians 1:16-21 contradicts Acts 9:20-30.

    a. Galatians 1:16-21 says Paul went to Arabia and then back to Damascus for a total of three years before going to Jerusalem. Galatians 1:18 says that after the three years Paul went to Jerusalem and spent 15 days with "... Peter only save Jamnes the brother of Jesus.

b. Acts 9:26 makes it sound as though Paul went immediately to Jerusalem from Damascus. Acts 9:27 says that Barnabas took Paul to the apostles 28. "And he was with <u>them</u> coming in and going out at Jerusalem." This should mean <u>most all</u> the apostles or at least most of them.

CONTRADICTION: In one place Paul says it was three years before he saw the Apostles. Luke makes it sound as though Paul went right away to see the Apostles.

SOLUTION: His whole point in Galatians is to show that his gospel teachings are straight from Jesus Christ and have nothing to do with man or even Jesus Christ's apostles. Why the contradiction? I haven't any idea and can't find any comment on it.

15. <u>1 Timothy 6:16 contradicts about everything: "Who only hath immortality." speaking of Jesus Christ.</u>

CONTRADICTION: "Here is an obvious error in the King James Version of the Bible. To assert that Christ only has immortality is to run counter to the whole doctrine of the resurrection." Elder Bruce R. McConkie, DNTC 3:95 This doctrine is stated many times in the New Testament.

SOLUTION: Joseph Smith clarified 1 Timothy 6:16 to read, "Whom no man hath seen, nor can see, unto whom no man can approach, only he who hath the light and the hope of immortality dwelling in him.

16. <u>Ephesians 4:26 contradicts Ephesians 4:31 plus many others.</u>

    a. Ephesians 4:26 says, "<u>Be ye angry</u>, and sin not; let not the sun go down upon your wrath.

    b. Ephesians 4:31. Just five verses later, Paul says, "Let all bitterness, and wrath, and <u>anger</u>, and clamour, and evil speaking, be put away from you, with all malice."

SOLUTION: Joseph corrected Ephesians 4:26 to read, "Can ye be angry, and not sin? Let not the sun go down upon your wrath:

17. <u>Hebrews 6:1 contradicts itself.</u>

    a. Hebrews 6:1 says, "Therefore leaving the principles of the doctrine of Christ, let us go on unto perfection:..." One can't <u>leave</u> or set aside the principles of the doctrine of Christ and go on to perfection.

SOLUTION: Joseph Smith said, "I will render it as it should be-"Therefore not leaving the principles of the doctrine of Christ, let us go on unto perfection, not laying again the foundation of repentance from dead works, and of faith toward God, of the doctrine of baptisms, and of laying on of hands, and of resurrection of the dead, and of eternal judgement.""" (Joseph Smith, **Teachings**, p. 328) Not terribly clear but certainly no longer a contradiction. As Peter says in 2 Peter 3:16, (speaking of Paul) "As also in all his epistles, speaking in them of these things; ("these things" refer to the Second Coming and Salvation) <u>in which are some things hard to be understood..."</u> Yes, some things in Paul's letters are hard to understand and part of it is certainly due to incorrect translation and omissions. But even Peter had trouble understanding Paul's writings before the omissions and incorrect translations took place!

18. <u>Hebrews 7:3 contradicts the laws of reproduction and life as set forth by God.</u>

   a. Hebrews 7:3 says, in talking about Melchizedek, king of Salem, priest of the most high God, "Without father, without mother, without descent, having neither beginning of days, nor end of life; but made like unto the Son of God; abideth a priest continually." This defies all laws of this world regarding Man, his creation, his mortality.

SOLUTION: Joseph Smith cleared it up in the Inspired Version: "For this Melchizedek was ordained a priest after the order of the Son of God, <u>which order</u> was without father, without mother, without descent, having neither beginning of days, nor end of life. And all those who are ordained unto this priesthood are made like unto the Son of God, abiding a priest continually." Clears up the contradiction beautifully-it is the order of the priesthood and not the parentage of Melchizedek that Paul was talking about. The Levitical Priesthood did have parentage, ie., from father to son.

19. Some other contradictions are: 2 Sam 24:11 and 1 Chr 21:1; 2 Kgs 8:26 and 2 Chr 22:2; Jer 34:4-5 and Jer 52:10-11; 2 Sam 10:18 and 1 Chr 19:18.

We hope the reader will understand and appreciate our motive. It is not to simply find fault with the Holy Bible but to offer the solutions to the contradictions that have occurred through mistranslations which are totally honest errors.

CHAPTER 23

Questions Regarding the Church of Jesus Christ of Latter Day Saints

1. <u>Does God have a physical body or is He an essence (or mist) as described by Eusebius, Bishop of Caesarea in 325 AD and believed by most churches today?</u>

    1. Genesis 1:26-27 says, "And God said, Let us make man in our image, after our likeness..." If God is an essence or a mist, are we then little mists? No, we are real as God is real.

    2. Genesis 5:3 The same manner of description is used by Moses to describe Adam's son, Seth: "...and begat a son in his own likeness, after his image,..."

    3. John 14:9 Jesus says, "...he that hath seen me hath seen the Father;..." Many saw Jesus Christ so Jesus is saying they look exactly alike.

4. Paul, who was caught up into the Third Heaven, 2 Corinthians 12:2, and obviously saw God and Jesus Christ as he testified in Hebrews 1:3, Romans 8:34 and 2 Corinthians 4:4.

5. James also taught the same doctrine in James 3:9 when he said that we are "...made after the similitude of God." Rulon Howell, in his book, "In His Many Mansions", states that we are the only church that teaches this doctrine today. The way he compiled the book was by writing to the different churches and asking the leaders to state their beliefs on a number of subjects, such as does God have a body.

6. Joseph Smith saw God and Jesus Christ as separate personages in the Sacred Grove, just south of Palmyra, New York in the spring of 1820. On April 2, 1843, Joseph testified, "The Father has a body of flesh and bones as tangible as man's: (quickened by spirit and not by blood) the Son also (Luke 24:39); but the Holy Ghost has not a body of flesh and bones, but is a personage of Spirit. were it not so, the Holy Ghost could not dwell in us." D&C 130:22.

2. <u>Why is the baptismal prayer in the Book of Mormon, 3 Nephi 11:25, different than the one we use today., D&C 20:732</u>

1. The difference is that one uses the word "authority" and the other uses the word "commissioned". They mean

almost exactly the same thing except commissioned is a little more explanatory and requires a person to have evidence of his authority. That is why we encourage missionaries to carry their line of authority card. This card will trace their authority back to Jesus Christ.

3. Why do we have so many High Priests? Wasn't there only one High Priest on the earth at a time? Wasn't Jesus the last High Priest on the earth?

   1. It is easy to confuse the Presiding High Priest with High Priests. Jesus was the Presiding High Priest of His Church in the early days as He is the Presiding High Priest of His Church (The Church of Jesus Christ of Latter Day Saints) today. Currently, President Nelson is the Presiding High Priest of His Church on the earth. The Bishop is the Presiding High Priest of his ward. The Stake President is the Presiding High Priest of the stake.

   2. By divine revelation received at various times the Melchizedek Priesthood with its offices of Elder, Seventy and High Priest was restored to the earth in June, 1829, never to be taken from the earth again. You will see that even in the beginning there were more than one High Priest but only one Presiding HighPriest of the Church.

4. Are there scriptures in the Bible that reinforce the doctrine of a pre-mortal life or what we call pre-existence?

1. Yes, many. Among them are: Proverbs Chapter 8; Ecclesiastes 12:7; Jeremiah 1:5; John 3:13; Ephesians 1:4-5; 2 Timothy 1:9; Titus 1:2; Hebrews 1:2; Jude 1:6.
   2. Let's see what the Another Testament of Jesus Christ says: Alma 13:3; Helaman 14:17.
   3. There are numerous scriptures in D&C and Pearl of Great Price. See Topical Guide: Man, Antemortal Existence; Spirit Creation.

5. <u>If the Book of Mormon has the fullness of the Gospel, why do we need the Bible?</u>

   1. 1 Nephi 13:21-23 and 39-42; 2 Nephi 29:3-9; Mormon 7:8-9.

6. <u>If the Bible had the fullness of the Gospel, what happened to it?</u>

   1. In Galatians 1st chapter, Paul is lamenting the fact that the Gospel was already being perverted in his day by the Judaizers. 1 Nephi 13:26-30

7. <u>Why can't I worship to or through the Virgin Mary or the Saints? (referring to the Catholic definition of the word Saints)</u>

   1. Exodus 20: 3-5 No gods before me-No graven image-thou shall not bow down before them; Deut. 6:14 No

other gods; Leviticus 19:4 No idols; John 14:6 Jesus only is the mediator; 1 Timothy 2:5 One mediator, Jesus Christ-so we can't use Mary as a mediator: Mosiah 3:17 Jesus is the only name through which salvation is given; D&C 93:19 Worship the Father in my name (Jesus talking).

8. <u>In the Bible (Ephesians 2:5) and the Book of Mormon (2 Nephi 25:23) it says that by grace are we saved. Why do you think we need works to save us?</u>

   1. First, we must define what is meant in these two instances by "saved". Saved from what? In Ephesians 2:1 Paul tells us, "And you hath he quickened (made alive) who were dead in trespasses and sins. Then in verse 8 he says, "For by grace (gift) are ye saved (from trespasses and sins) through faith; and that not of yourselves; it is the gift of God: (through the Atonement of Jesus Christ: verse 9. Not of works (This was in rebuttal to the "Judaizers") lest any man should boast." This is one of the most misinterpreted scriptures in the New Testament. They don't read it with Ephesians 2:1, instead just interpret it to mean that all they have to do is believe to be saved in the kingdom of Heaven, no matter how many sins they commit. If they are correct, why did Paul spend the entire chapter 6 telling people to be good? Or why, in the preceding book, Galatians 6:4-5, did Paul say, "But let every man prove his own work,

and then shall he have rejoicing in himself alone, and not in another, For every man shall bear his own burden." and in 7. "Be not deceived; God is not mocked; for whatsoever a man soweth, that shall he also reap."

2. 2 Nephi 25:26 explains 2 Nephi 25:23 the same way.

3. Also Romans 2:13, James 2:14-26 point out rather well that being saved (according to Ephesians 2:8) will not put us into Father's presence. See also Matthew 16:27; Luke 6:46-49; Romans 2:13 & 21-24;2 Nephi 10:24; Alma 22:14.

9. <u>How is it that only those who marry in the temple receive the greatest glory in the Celestial Kingdom when Paul wrote to the Corinthians in 1 Corinthians 7:6-9.</u>

1. Paul was not talking about the Celestial Kingdom. He was saying it is better to be like him (single and celibate) but note verse 6: "I speak this by permission, and not by commandment." ie., this was Paul's opinion and not a commandment of the Lord. He went on to say in 9, "But if they cannot contain (use self-control) it is better to marry than to burn (burn with lust)"

2. When Joseph Smith Jr sought help of God, in dealing with the Shakers who had become members of the Church, some of whom thought that living single and celibate was a higher form of living than marriage. D&C 49:15 says "Forbidding to marry is not of God."

QUESTIONS REGARDING THE CHURCH OF JESUS CHRIST

10. <u>Some members of the Church try to use the 89th Section to say we should be virtually vegetarians. Should we be?</u>

    1. No. D&C 49:18-19 says "And whoso forbiddeth to abstain from meats...is not ordained of God;" but warned on wasting in D&C 49:21.

11. <u>Why can't we drink coffee when we drink hot chocolate? Both contain caffeine.</u>

    1. Caffeine also is in colas as well and it definitely is addictive. That is why it is placed in colas. We have been counseled by the First Presidency not to partake of anything that is addictive. However, there is very little caffeine in hot chocolate compared to coffee and I have never heard of anyone being addicted to hot chocolate compared to the millions who are addicted to coffee, tea, colas or other caffeine drinks.

    2. In the 1960's and confirmed in the 1980's was found something far worse than caffeine in coffee and tea- Cadmium. This is a rare earth metal that gets into the blood vessels, scores (abrades) them, causing cholesterol clots which in turn causes high blood pressure and obstruction of vital blood vessels.

    Tea has a strong kidney stimuli called Theobromine. That is why tea is given to patients in the hospital, to help them to urinate. However, in heavy tea drinkers it can lead to gradual kidney failure and death.

While I served as a Bishop a couple were thinking about joining the Church. The husband, Roy Smith, told me he was having trouble about giving up tea. "My folks have always been heavy tea drinkers, consuming as much as a gallon a day." "Oh, so they have had bad kidney problems", I said. I couldn't have hit him with a cattle prod and shocked him any more. He then proceeded to tell me of how his grandfather, his uncle and other relatives had died of kidney failure. His father was currently on dialysis and died a year later. They had never been told that the tea was killing them. He joined and they were great members.

3. Coffee and tea also contain minute amounts of tannin, used in dyes and tanning of hides. It has an astringent effect and continued use may cause stomach disorders.

4. The only ones that will keep us from going to the temple are coffee and tea. However, we should heed the advice of the First Presidency and leave them all alone.

12. I have been baptized already. Why do I need to be baptized again?

1. First, there is the matter of authority. Can we assume it? Paul says absolutely not in Acts 19:1-6. These 12 men had been baptized by John and if ever there was a pure man who could assume that he had the authority it would have been John the Baptist. No one could

doubt his educational background as he was taught by Heavenly angels.

2. I can show my Line of Authority which traces back to Jesus Christ which gives me the authority to baptize and perform other ordinances. Does any other church have it? That is the beauty of the Restoration. See also 3 Nephi 11:21-28; D&C 22:1-4; D&C 39:5-15.

13. <u>Do angels have wings as depicted in most famous Christian paintings?</u>

   1. No. Acts 10:3, 30. "A man stood before me in bright clothing." No description of wings. If there had been they would have been mentioned.

   2. John 20:12 "Two angels in white sitting". If something as prominent as wings had been present you can bet they would have stated it. See Topical Guide for many more.

   3. Probably, the very scripture that we use to talk about Moroni (Revelations 14:6) may be the reason for wings on angels as John said he saw an angel "...fly in the midst of heaven,...". Obviously there are other ways of flying without wings which the early artists did not understand. I'm surprised they haven't put wings on Christ at the Ascension!

14. <u>Was the Book of Mormon translated by the gift and power of God?</u>

1. When Joseph Smith, Jr translated the Book of Mormon he was 24 years old with a third grade education. Some of his early letters show he couldn't spell very well. Later his widow, Emma Hale Smith, said that at that time (1829) he couldn't even write or dictate a good letter, much less translate the Book of Mormon. She called it a marvel and a wonder, in other words a miracle.

2. He translated the plates in approximately 75 days from a very different language from English. It took 5-6 scholars almost three years to translate the Book of Mormon from English to Spanish which are very similar languages, both deriving most of their words from Latin.

3. Lest anyone take the Book of Mormon lightly, ask them to read Moroni 10:27-29. If they shall read the Book of Mormon and scoff at it, it shall be a witness against them at the Day of Judgement! That should make the hardest of hearts have second thoughts before scoffing!!

15. <u>How can we know whether Joseph Smith, Jr was a prophet or not?</u>

　1. The main responsibility of a prophet is to be a forth-teller rather than a foreteller. In other words, one who calls the people to repentance.

　2. A seer is one who sees into the past and the future and prophecies, a foreteller . (Mosiah 8:15-17)

3. We sustain Joseph as Prophet, Seer and Revelator. One of the ways we can know if Joseph is a true prophet and seer is to see if his prophecies came true. See Prophecies of Joseph Smith, Jr of his foretelling over which he had no control as to the outcome. Another way is to pray but remember D&C 9:7 & 8. You must first study, Asking alone, for most people, will not get it. It sure didn't for Oliver Cowdery.

16. The Bible is good enough for me. It contains all of God's word.

    1. John 21:25 The world could not contain all the books if all of the words and works of Jesus Christ were written. Nobody would dare to say that those words or works are any less important!
    2. There are 14 books missing from the Bible. See Lost books in the Bible Dictionary.
    3. Philippians 4:8 We should seek after additional truths and additional witnesses such as the Book of Mormon.
    4. Acts 20:35 Jesus said, "..It is more blessed to give than to receive." This great truism is never stated in the Four Gospels by Jesus. Also the prophecy in Matthew 2:23 regarding Jesus being a Nazarene is not found in the Old Testament. How many other precious truths are missing?

Are the Mormons Teaching Fables

5. 2 Corinthians 13:1 Paul states that this is the third letter to the people of Corinth so the first letter is lost (1 Corinthians 5:9). If the other two are considered God's word, this one should also be. Another of Paul's lost epistles is mentioned in Colossians 4:16.

6. 2 Nephi 29:3-8 Wherefore murmur ye, because that ye shall receive more of my word? He can't believe it!

17. <u>I believe in Christ, I don't see any need to go to church and do all that stuff. Christ didn't recognize a church.</u>

   1. Oh yes he did. Matthew 18:17 recognized the church. Matthew 16:18 I will build my church. Ephesians 2:20 Jesus was the chief cornerstone of the Church.

18. <u>Is there a God or not? Let's see what some of the greatest scientific minds of our time have said.</u>

   1. Albert Einstein: This world is so complex and organized that it had to have at its helm A Supreme Being or a Creator.

   2. Werner Von Braun-Director of our Space program for many years: Matter is never lost, it simply changes form so life goes on. Matter had to have a creator, an organizer. See D&C 93:33

   3. Farnsworth-Inventor of TV from Rigby, Idaho: The likelihood of this world and man having evolved is the

same likelihood of a print shop exploding and having all the type fall back to the ground in the form of Webster's Dictionary.

4. Moroni 10:3-5 James 1:5-6 Ask them to pray about it and report their feelings.

5. Another very excellent method is the one of reliable witnesses: Adam in Moses 5:10; Enoch in Moses 7:69; Noah in Genesis 6:9; Noah, Shem, Ham & Japheth in Moses 8:27; Abram-meaning exalted father (later changed to Abraham-meaning father of a multitude) in Genesis 17:1 and Abraham 3:11; Jacob in Genesis 32:30; Seventy-four people saw God in Exodus 24:9-10!; Moses in Exodus 33:11, Deuteronomy 34:10 & Moses 1:2 & 11; Manoah and his wife (parents of Samson) in Judges 13:22; Solomon in 1 Kings 11:9; Isaiah in Isaiah 6:5; Stephen in Acts 7:56; Paul in 2 Corinthians 12:2 & Hebrews 1:3; Joseph in JS-H 1:17; Joseph and Sidney in D&C 76:23.

19. <u>Why are there wars? Why do people get sick and die early? Why are people killed by cars and airplane crashes in the prime of their life? If there is a God, wouldn't He prevent them if He loved us?</u>

1. He does love us and that is why He allows us the free agency to choose our own steps rather than making us robots as Satan would have us do. Satan seeketh that all

men might be miserable like unto himself (Devil). See James 4:1-10, showing disobedience to God. See Moses 4:1-4. Not a soul would be lost. But the reason is found in 2 Nephi 2:27 He causes wars. See 2 Nephi 2:15-16. If we have free agency then there must be opposition in all things. On the other hand, see 2 Peter 3:9 and Alma 14:10-11.

2. In the creation of the world certain physical laws were established, such as gravity, mass and force. Step in front of a car going 60 mph and splat!

3. God wants us to return to his presence and become like Him, knowing good from evil, and choosing good, etc. See Agency in Mormon Doctrine. We can choose and study good health by proper exercise and nutrition or we can choose to remain ignorant and suffer the degenerative diseases.

4. See D&C 121:7-Thy afflictions will be but a moment. Also D&C 122:7-9 Thy afflictions are for our good and cannot compare with the afflictions of our Savior.

20. <u>Do Momons believe in Christ? (See #19 as well)</u>

1. The name of the Church is the Church of Jesus Christ (3 Nephi 27:8) of Latter Day Saints as compared with the Church of Jesus Christ of Former Day Saints established by Jesus Christ and taught by Paul.

2. Read the Articles of Faith, 1-13.

QUESTIONS REGARDING THE CHURCH OF JESUS CHRIST

3. Acts 16:3 "...this Jesus I preach unto you is Christ.", says Paul. That is what we testify and teach.

4. We believe The Book of Mormon, translated by the gift and power of God, to be Another Testament of Christ.

5. The word Christ (or a similar word) is used approximately the following number of times: Old Testament-36 times; New Testament-654 times; Book of Mormon-468 times; Doctrine & Covenants-169 times; Pearl of Great Price-18 times.

6. 2 Nephi 25:26 says, "And we talk of Christ, we rejoice in Christ, we preach of Christ, we prophesy of Christ,..."

That should be clear enough, shouldn't it??

21. <u>Revelations 22:18 is very plain that we can't add to nor take away from "this book". How can you justify adding to this book by believing in the Book of Mormon?</u>

1. First of all "this book" refers to the Book of Revelations, not to the Bible. The Book of Revelations was written approximately in 95 AD, according to Bible scholars. John wrote 1,2 & 3 John in approximately 96 AD or later., according to the same scholars. Understand that the Bible was separate books or epistles (letters) until the second century AD and has been rearranged several times since.

2. The word Bible is taken from the Greek word ta biblia which means the books. Note the plural. Everyone

refers to the Book of John or the Book of Matthew, etc., so the Bible is a collection of books.

3. By the time John wrote the Book of Revelations, scholars say there had been some tampering with some of the writings of Peter, James and Paul. John was trying to scare them off.

4. Moses did the same thing in Deuteronomy 4:2 which would mean we should forget all writings but Moses, using the same logic.

22. <u>Are Mormons Christians?</u>

In order to best answer the question, we must first define the word, Christian. Elder Bruce R. McConkie says:

1. If Christians are people with the defined view that salvation comes only through the complete gospel of Christ, Mormons are truly Christians in the precise and full meaning of the term.

2. If Christians are defined as people (and this is the standard definition of the clergy of the day) who believe in the holy trinity as defined and set forth in the Nicene, Athanasian, and Apostles creeds, meaning that God is a three-in-one nothingness, a spirit essence filling immensity, an incorporeal (without a body) and uncreated being incapable of definition or mortal comprehension-then Mormons, by a

QUESTIONS REGARDING THE CHURCH OF JESUS CHRIST

clergy-chosen definition, are ruled out of the fold of Christ.

3. If Christians are defined as the saints of God in Antioch and elsewhere who believe and live as they did; if by Christians is meant those who accept Christ as the literal Son of God; who believe that miracles and signs follow true believers; who believe in kingdoms of glory, revelation, the gathering of Israel, and Melchizedek and Aaronic Priesthoods; who believe there must.be apostles and prophets in the Church; and who believe in all respects as did holy men of old-then Mormons are Christians. Indeed, Mormonism is pure, unadulterated Christianity, restored anew in all its grandeur and glory. See Alma 46:13-16 also.

23. <u>What is meant by the Nicene Creed?</u>

1. The Nicene Council composed of approximately 318 bishops (says Eusebius) of the Catholic (the word catholic means universal) Church met in 325 AD to try to decide what Jesus Christ was made of. Sounds silly? Sure it is. But Emperor Constantine, emperor of the Roman empire, who felt that God had helped him win his battle over Licinius in 323 AD and espoused the Christian cause, called the conference or council (in fact paid for all their expenses) and sent for the bishops from all over the then known Christian world to come to Nicea, in Bithynia on the south border of the Black Sea (in Turkey today) and

settle "once and for all time" the question of whether Jesus Christ, (since God "obviously" was the ethereal God that could be in your shirt pocket or surround the whole world-a mist) was a break-off of this substance of which God was made or was he made from nothing? Absurd as it sounds, there was a terrible division within the Church as to which was right, each side trying to arouse their followers and succeeding in a great agitation, causing a civil war within the church. The "substance" believers excommunicated the "nothing" believers!

Another issue was on what day that Easter was to be celebrated. Big division.

2. Emperor Constantine of the Holy Roman Empire stated in his opening remarks to the Council, "An internal sedition in the Church is, in my apprehension, more dangerous and formidable than any war in which I can be engaged;" He then acted as mediator, speaking in both Latin and Greek, trying to get the two sides to agree, feeling that agreement was more important than truth. As we now know, both sides were wrong anyway so he was correct in trying to promote harmony.

24. What is the actual Nicene Creed?

1. After days of wrangling, with many heated debates, exactly one month later, August 25, 325 AD, almost all 318 bishops signed the Nicene Creed:

"We believe in one God, the Father Almighty, Maker of all things, visible and invisible; and in one Lord Jesus Christ, the Son of God, the only begotten of the Father, that is, of the substance of the Father (this was the subject of the terrible division-whether Jesus was made from part of the "mist" or "essence" of God or from nothing); God of Gods, light of light, true God of true God; begotten, not made, consubstantial (of the same substance) with the Father, by whom all things were made, both in heaven and earth; who for us men, (how about women??) and for our salvation, descended, (what about the virgin birth?) was incarnate (was in the flesh), and was made man, and suffered, and rose again the third day: he ascended into heaven, and shall come to judge the living and the dead: And in the Holy Spirit.

But the holy catholic (universal) and apostolic Church of God anathematized (cursed) those who affirm that there was a time when the Son was not, or that he was not before he was begotten (so they recognize preexistence??), or that he was made of things not existing; or who say, that the Son of God was of any other substance or essence, or created, or liable to change or conversion."

In writing about the Creed to the Church of Cesarea shortly after its adoption, Eusebius Pamphilus said:

(He had been the one that submitted the wording for the Creed except for the word, consubstantial, which was added as a compromise) "...But our pious emperor (Constantine) himself was the first to declare, that it (Eusebius' Creed) was extremely well conceived, and that it expressed his own sentiments, exhorting all to assent to, and sign it, that they might unite in its doctrines, with addition only of the single word consubstantial (of the same substance).....and that the Son did not subsist from the Father, either by division or abscission (by being cut off from the mist or essence- can you imagine such a belief??) since it was impossible that an immaterial, intellectual and incorporeal nature could admit of any bodily affection: but that it must be understood in a divine and mysterious manner. (This is the definition of God by the most important and persuasive bishop that existed in the Catholic (universal) Church in 325 AD, just 250 years after some of the scriptures quoted above were written!!) Did Paul's prophecy to the people of Thessalonica (2 Thessalonians 2:2-3) come true when he said that there must be a falling away first for Jesus' second coming? See also 2 Timothy 4:3. Does this help you understand why there had to be a restoration not just a reformation of the Gospel?

25. <u>What is a "BORN AGAIN" Christian? (See #22)</u>We have already discussed whether we are Christians. We are, according to our definition of what a Christian is. We need to know it so that we can define the difference to a questioner who is a non-member. Now let's look at the meaning of "born again" to see if we qualify:

1. What is "born again" taken to mean by some?

    a. That you believe in Jesus Christ and in him crucified and that is all that is necessary. Go on and live whatever life you choose to live-evil or good-it is okay. It is not necessary to attend church. After all, that is where the hypocrites dwell!.

    b. That you believe in Jesus Christ and in him crucified, rose from the grave, and took upon Himself all your sins. You must be baptized in a particular church to qualify to be a "born again" Christian. Simply because you believe and are baptized, you will want to do good-well, at least most of the time-well, at least some of the time! But it's okay, Christ died for your sins anyway. So, you are all set for life with an automatic ticket to heaven! (Wow, what a convenient religion! Sounds like "...the philosophies of men mingled with the Scriptures". I used to think that this was all there was to religion!)

What should "born again" mean? Let's let the scriptures tell us:

a. John 3:3-7 Jesus answered (Nicodemus of the Sanhedrin who came by night) and said unto him, Verily, verily I say unto thee, Except a man be born again, he cannot see the kingdom of God. (He then went on to explain that we must be baptized by water and by the spirit, ie., receive the Gift of the Holy Ghost)

b. 2 Timothy 4:6-8. We must fight the good fight, that is keep the commandments. We must be good.

c. Philippians 3: "..Christ Jesus my Lord; for whom I have suffered the loss of all things, and do count them but dung, that I may win Christ." We must have a mighty change in our lives and be willing to give up all bad things to win Christ.

d. Alma 5:14. This makes it much clearer: And now behold, I ask of you, my brethren of the church, have ye spiritually been born of God? (Born again) Have ye received his image in your countenances? Have ye experienced this mighty change in your hearts?

e. Mosiah 27:24-25 For, said he, I have repented of my sins, and have been redeemed of the Lord; behold I am born of the Spirit. 25. And the Lord said unto me: Marvel not that all mankind, yea, men and women, all nations, kindreds, tongues and people, must be born again: yea, born of God, changed from their carnal and fallen state, to a state of righteousness, being redeemed of God, becoming his sons and daughters; 26. And thus they become new creatures; and unless they do this, they can in nowise inherit the kingdom of God. Are you, as a temple-recommend-carrying member of the Church of Jesus Christ of Latter Day Saints, a "born again Christian "? Yes, definitely!

Let's say you are a "born again" Christian under our understanding in #2 above. Are you all set for life? Let's go further. Let's say you do all the outward ordinances of the restored gospel-you are baptized, men receiving the Priesthood, receive your endowments, go on a mission, be married or sealed in the Temple for time and all eternity. Are you now all set for life with an automatic ticket to heaven?? Surely all that should suffice!

a. Matthew 10:22, 24:13, Mark 13:13. "But he that shall endure (persevere-is steadfast in keeping the commandments) unto the end, the same shall be saved." In other words we must keep the commandments and do the teachings of the prophets, both olden times and present, unto the end of our lives in order to be saved or to be with Elohim. As Paul says in 2 Timothy 4:6-8, we must fight the good fight and keep the faith to the end in order to receive a crown of righteousness. By the way, don't confuse this "saved" with Paul's meaning of "saved" in Ephesians 2:8 where Paul is talking about being saved from death and sin and not about being with Heavenly Father again.

b. Furthermore, if we have been given much such as all the blessings mentioned in 4. and cease living the Gospel we may wish the earth would fall down upon us for we will be judged by the higher laws we have been given with its higher reward, the Celestial Kingdom. See D&C 82:3 and 7.

c. See also 1 Corinthians 6:9 and Alma 24:30

26. Is Jehovah of the Old Testament the same as Jesus Christ?

   1. Isaiah 43:11 then Acts 4:10-12
   2. Hosea 13:4 then Luke 2:11
   3. Isaiah 12:10 to Acts 4:12
   4. Zechariah 12:10 to John 19:37 to Isaiah 44:6
   5. 3 Nephi 15:5. Jesus gave the law so He would surely be the Jehovah.

27. Why do we celebrate the Sabbath on Sunday?

   See SABBATH & SUNDAY by Glenn R. Orr

28. <u>Why is baptism by immersion necessary? I was sprinkled and I have always believed that it was all the same.</u>

   1. John baptized in the river Jordan (Mark 1:5). Matthew 3:16 "Jesus...went up straightway out of the water" after being baptized by John in the river Jordan. If sprinkling was all that was necessary they could have done that in Jerusalem.

   2. In Acts 8:38, Luke tells us of Philip baptizing the eunuch: "And he (the eunuch) commanded the chariot to stand still: and they went down both into the water, both Philip and the eunuch; and he (Philip) baptized him (the eunuch)." You don't go down into the water to sprinkle, you bury them in the water,, as Paul taught.

   3. In Colossians 2:12 Paul teaches, "Buried with him (Jesus Christ) in baptism wherein also ye are risen with him through the faith of the operation of God, who hath raised him (Jesus Christ) from the dead."

   4. In Romans 6:4 Paul teaches, "Therefore we are buried with him by baptism into death: that like as Christ was raised up from the dead by the glory of the Father, even so we also should walk in newness of life."

   5. Mosiah 18:14 "...were buried in the water."

   6. 3 Nephi 11:26 "...immerse them in the water."

   7. 3 Nephi 19:13 (following baptism) "...had come up out of the water.

8. D&C 20:74 "...immerse him or her in the water." D&C 76:50-53 states it clearly.

   9. See Articles of Faith #4

29. <u>Then what does Ezekiel 36:25 mean when it talks about sprinkling with clean water? Isn't that baptism?</u>

   1. Look in the Topical Guide under "Sprinkle" and you will see that the practice started with Moses (read Exodus 24:38 to get the context) and it is a sign of the covenant made with God by the covenant people. It later (Ezekiel 36:25) was used with water as a sign of the covenant and of cleansing. Paul then refers to it in (Hebrews 12:24) as a sign of the new covenant as does Peter (1 Peter 1:2). So it has to do with the covenant of keeping the commandments but not to the act of baptism. Otherwise the scriptures would be contradictory and they are not in this instance.

30. <u>How do we explain Brigham Young's statement that has been interpreted that we Mormons believe that Adam is our God?</u>

   1. For a complete answer see Doctrines of Salvation, Vol I, pp 96-106, also Mormon Doctrine, Adam-God Theory.

   2. He is "supposed" to have said about Adam, "He is our father and our God, and the only God with whom we have to do." If we just read the rest of the discourse

without referring to other discourses, we can see that this was transcribed wrong. Before this statement, Brigham Young said of Adam, "He helped to make and organize this world." In other words, there was a Being superior to Adam who organized this world. In the same discourse President Young says, "It is true that the earth was organized by three distinct characters, namely Elohim, Jehovah, and Michael." We know that Michael is Adam so he places him third in importance and also in the same discourse says, "Then the Lord by his power and wisdom organized the mortal tabernacle of man." Who was the first man? Adam.

Young is correctly stating (according to all the other scriptures such as Genesis 3:22) that Elohim created Adam. The same old story: The Antis mix a little bit of truth with a lot of falsehoods and mess up the minds of those who won't take the time to study it.

31. Is baptism really necessary?

   1. John 3:5
   2. Matthew 3:13-15. If it was necessary to fulfill all righteousness for Jesus, it should be necessary for us!
   3. D&C 18:42 All need to repent and be baptized.

32. D&C 84:19-22. Is this saying we must hold the Melchizedek Priesthood in order to see God?

1. This is not talking about seeing God. It is talking about the power to give blessings in the name of God. In other words the power of the Priesthood is not manifest (available) unless we hold the Melchizedek Priesthood. See D&C 67:11 for what is required to see God.

33. <u>Why can women not be sealed to more than one husband?</u>

   1. God's house is a house of order and there are certain rules and commandments we do not fully understand, yet we sustain them. He established on this earth a patriarchal society and we need to abide by this rule. God has a pattern or plan in all things. D&C 52:14.

34. <u>How is it that in the first part of D&C 29, Jesus is talking about Himself and the Father and in the last part it sounds like the Father is talking about Mine Only Begotten or Jesus?</u>

   1. It is called Divine Investiture of Authority which means since he is one with the Father in all of the attributes of perfection, and since he exercises the power and authority of the Father, it follows that everything he says or does is and would be exactly and precisely what the Father would say and do under the same circumstances. Mormon Doctrine, p 130

   2. Jesus can also be termed the Father in the sense that He is the Creator of this world. He can also be called the Father in the sense of all who follow Him who are born again.

QUESTIONS REGARDING THE CHURCH OF JESUS CHRIST

35. <u>How come the writings of Isaiah in the Book of Mormon and the writings of Isaiah in the King James Version are almost identical?</u>

   1. Actually there are 199 verses that are the same but 234 verses are different. According to Ludlow he theorizes, "When Joseph translated the Isaiah references from the Small plates of Nephi, he evidently opened his King James Version of the Bible and compared the impression he had received in translating with the words of the King James scholars. If his translation was essentially the same as that of the King James Version, he apparently quoted the verse from the Bible; then his scribe, Oliver Cowdery, copied it down. However., if Joseph's translation did not agree precisely, he would dictate his to Oliver. Although some may question this procedure, scholars today used the same procedure to translate the Dead Sea Scrolls." Makes sense. See Joseph Smith-History 1:36-41 where some differences in the King James Version are noted by Moroni.

36. <u>In 1 Corinthians 11:1-15 the woman was not to pray with head uncovered ie., she was to have a hat on. She was to have long hair and the man not. Should this be the custom today?</u>

   1. According to Elder Bruce R. McConkie in Doctrinal New Testament Vol I, p 361, Paul was citing local

custom which was that an uncovered head was "...as if her head was shaven." which would indicate that she was an adulteress.

In Paul's day a bare head was a sign of irreverence. Today, a bare head is a sign of reverence, especially with men. In the eternal sense it is wholly immaterial.

37. <u>Do we really need to pray?</u>

  1. Alma 13:27-30 Pray continually. Alma 37:36-37 says the same.
  2. 2 Nephi 32:8 Evil Spirit teacheth man not to pray.
  3. 3 Nephi 18:15 Pray always lest ye be tempted of the devil.
  4. D&C 10:5 and 75:11 Praying always.

38. <u>Some say that you should pray before giving a blessing or administering to someone. Is that true?</u>

  1. 2 Nephi 32:9 "Not perform any thing unto the Lord save in the first place ye shall pray..."
  2. James 5:14 "...Let them pray over him" and then it says to anoint him with oil.

39. <u>Why is your church called "Latter Day Saints", why not just The Church of Jesus Christ? Furthermore, what is the need now for apostles and prophets?</u>

QUESTIONS REGARDING THE CHURCH OF JESUS CHRIST

1. Paul teaches in Ephesians 4:11-12, "And he (Jesus Christ) gave some, apostles; and some, prophets; and some, evangelists; and some, pastors and teachers; For the perfecting of the saints, (followers of Jesus Christ- That is why we are called the Church of Jesus Christ of Latter Day Saints, to distinguish us from the early day saints or what is called the Primitive Church) for the work of the ministry, for the edifying of the body (Church) of Christ:" Paul went on in verse 14 to tell the purpose of these offices, "That we henceforth be no more children, tossed to and fro, and carried about with every wind of doctrine, by the sleight of men, and cunning craftiness, whereby they lie in wait to deceive:" So the purpose of prophets and apostles is to keep us on the right path if we will listen and do!

2. Paul teaches in 1 Corinthians 12:28 the same thing, "And God hath set some in the church, first apostles, secondarily prophets, thirdly teachers.."

3. In Ephesians 2:19-20 Paul says of the saints at Ephesus that they are of the (in 19)"...household (church) of God;

   20. And are built upon the foundation of the apostles and prophets, Jesus Christ himself being the chief cornerstone:"

40. <u>Baptism is mentioned in the Book of Mormon in about 550 BC but is not mentioned in the Old Testament. Did baptism exist before John The Baptist and Jesus Christ only on the American Continent?</u>

Are the Mormons Teaching Fables

1. Latter-day Saint scriptures indicate that the history of this ordinance predates the ministry of John the Baptist. Beginning with Adam (Moses 6:64-66) baptism by immersion in water was introduced as standard practice, and has been observed in all subsequent dispensations of the gospel when priesthood authority was on the earth (D&C 20:25-27; 84:27-28).

2. Elder McConkie says in Mormon Doctrine (p. 71), "The Jews were baptizing their proselytes long before John, as is well attested from secular sources." In fact, their temple had a font resting upon 12 oxen and there are many places where the word washings appears in the Old Testament. (See Topical Guide-Washing) Baptism is a Greek word while washings is a Hebrew word for the same thing. Therefore, the word baptism would not appear in the Old Testament since the Old Testament was written in Hebrew.

3. Baptismal fonts exist in Central America today that probably predate the coming of Christ. Dr. P. De Roo (in about 1910) in "Americas Before Columbus" wrote: "Bishops Landa and Sahagun and other Spanish writers of that time (time of the Conquistadors-1520) assure us that baptism was administered in several American districts from time immemorial." The Indians (Lamanites) were still practicing it when the Spanish came.

41. <u>Jesus says in John 4:24 that God is a Spirit. Nothing about a body. Please explain that.</u>

   1. John has contradictions within the Book of John itself that lead one to conclude that there are several mistranslations: John 1:18 contradicts John 6:46 and John 14:21; John 4:2 contradicts John 3:22 and John 3:26. CONTRADICTIONS IN THE NEW TESTAMENT by Glenn R. Orr for more.

   2. Joseph Smith, Jr. corrected John 4:24 to read, "For unto such hath God promised his Spirit. And they who worship him, must worship in spirit and in truth." Makes a lot more sense.

   3. Luke 24:39 and then Hebrews 1:1-3 "...express image..."

   4. Acts 7:55-56

   5. D&C 130:22 Explains clearly

42. <u>Why is there a need for the Book of Mormon?</u>

   1. John 10:16 Other sheep have I

   2. Philippians 4:8 "...whatsoever things are true... honest... just.. pure. lovely... good report.. virtue... praise, think on these things."

   3. Matthew 4.4 "...Man cannot live by bread alone, but by every word that proceedeth out of the mouth of God."

Are the Mormons Teaching Fables

    4. 2 Corinthians 2:1 "In the mouth of two or three witnesses shall every word be established." The Bible is one- The Book of Mormon is the other.

    5. 2 Nephi 27:14 "..and in the mouth of as many witnesses as seemeth him good will he establish his word; and woe unto him that rejecteth the word of God!"

43. <u>Where does it say that parents will be able to raise their children in the millennium who have died in their infancy?</u>

    1. First, let's establish where the little children who die in infancy go. See D&C 137:10 They go to the Celestial Kingdom of Heaven. D&C 137: 10

    2. Second, do they need baptism to go to the Celestial Kingdom? No. See Moroni 8:5-26. When do they need to be baptized? If they die after the age of accountability which is anticipated to be eight years of age.

    3. How will the parents, in all the host of Heaven, make contact? By being sealed for time and all eternity, parent to children, in the Holy Temple. See Doctrines of Salvation, Vol I, p. 49-57.

    4. If they die after the age of 8 and have been baptized, should they be given their endowments even though they died, for example, at age 12? "Yes, they should receive their endowments by proxy because no blessing of Heaven will be denied them simply because they died early", says President Joseph Fielding

Smith in Doctrines of Salvation, Vol I, p 54. Isn't that exciting?

5. On page 55 President Smith says, "When a child is raised in the resurrection, the spirit will enter the body and the body will be the same size as it was when the child died. It will then grow after the resurrection to full maturity to conform to the size of the spirit." (as it was in the pre-existence)

6. On page 55 President Smith also says, "If parents are righteous (and have the children sealed to them), they will have their children after the resurrection. Little children who die, whose parents are not worthy of an exaltation, will be adopted into the families of those who are worthy."

44. <u>I'd believe in Joseph Smith but I don't feel the Lord appears to people in visions anymore.</u>

1. Joel 2:28

2. Amos 3:7 "Surely the Lord God will do nothing, but he revealeth his secret unto his servants the prophets."

3. Acts 2:17 "...in the last days I will pour out my Spirit, saith God and your sons and daughters shall prophesy and your young men shall see visions,..."

4. Malachi 3:6 I am the Lord, I cannot change

5. Mormon 9:19 "...And behold, I say unto you he changeth not; if so he would cease to be God; and he ceaseth not to be God.."

45. <u>I'm used to a cracker (wafer) and wine as a Sacrament. Bread and water seems a little strange to me.</u>

   1. It is all <u>symbolism</u> of the body and blood of Jesus Christ so what difference does it make? None.

   2. Soon after the organization of the Church in 1830, they were having trouble getting unfermented grape juice. So they enquired of the Lord what to do. D&C 27:1-5 was the answer.

46. <u>Let's say we join the Church and afterwards we sin. Why do we have to confess our sin to the Bishop?</u>

   1. How else would we start the road to repentance? We become members of the Church of Jesus Christ. It is His Church. The Bishop is ordained as a common judge in Israel of His Church. The Bishop sets the course of restitution necessary for the sin incurred. When we sin we are not only breaking the commandments but we are sinning against His Church. Don't confuse His Church with a social club. Membership must be taken seriously.

   2. D&C 58:17 To be a judge in Israel (of the Saints)

   3. D&C 107:68-75 "...to sit in judgment upon transgressors..

47. <u>What if I sin, then repent and then sin again? Can't I go right on sinning and repenting?</u>

1. Before long you will leave out the repenting part and Satan will have you because it gets harder to repent each time.

2. Hebrews 6:4-6 "For it is impossible for those who were once enlightened....if they shall fall away, to renew them again unto repentance; seeing they crucify to themselves the Son of God afresh,.."

3. D&C 82:3 Where much is given much is expected.

4. D&C 82:7 "...I say unto you sin no more...but unto that soul who sinneth (after repentance) shall the former sins return, saith the Lord your God."

48. <u>Some verses in the New Testament sound like God, Jesus and the Holy Ghost are one. Can you convince me from the New Testament that they are not one?</u>

   1. See ARE GOD AND JESUS ONE? by Glenn R. Orr. There are five verses that say God and Jesus are one. All can be explained if read in context to mean one in purpose, works, thought, word, deed, or looks. There are over 45 verses in the New Testament, Book of Mormon (remember-Another Testament of Jesus Christ!) that show they are separate personages.

49. <u>Should we pray out loud when having private prayer?</u>

   1. D&C 19:28 Must pray vocally as well as in secret.

2. D&C 20:47 The same

3. D&C 81:3 The same

50. <u>Why can't women hold the priesthood?</u>

   1. They hold something as precious-motherhood

   2. My wife says, "We don't need it, we have plenty of authority already!"

   3. God's house is a house of order and is a patriarchal society.

51. <u>Is there really a hell? Is it a state of mind or an actual place?</u>

   1. Yes, there really is a hell. It is both a state of mind and an actual place, according to which hell you are asking

   2. You really need to read Mormon Doctrine, Encyclopedia of Mormonism and our Bible Dictionary under "hell" to understand it.

   3. There are actually three parts or phases of hell:

      a. The hell on earth when we have sinned and are most miserable in our sins. Alma 38:18 This is the state of mind from which we can be saved by repentance.

      b. The hell those spirits experience after death (Spirit Prison-a place) who have not repented who must pay the "uttermost farthing"-to the last bit-for their sins. They will be taught by the Elders of the Church (both former and latter day elders) so that they can be judged with full knowledge of their sins. 1 Peter 4:6, D&C 138:34 These will be delivered up for judgment at the last judgment and, if they have paid for their sins will go to the telestial kingdom.

c. The hell reserved for the unrepentant who become the followers and teachers of the devil and includes the sons of perdition. This is an everlasting place of torment or Satan's kingdom. 2 Nephi 2:27-29

52. Where is the Garden of Eden?

1. President Joseph Fielding Smith in Doctrines of Salvation Vol II p. 74 says, "In accord with the revelations given to the Prophet Joseph Smith, we teach that the Garden of Eden was on the American continent where the City Zion, or the New Jerusalem, will be built. When Adam and Eve were driven out of the Garden, they eventually dwelt at a place called Adam-ondi-Ahman, situated in what is now Daviess County, Missouri."

2. Several years ago I took two bus loads of youth and sponsors on a Church History trip to Carthage and Nauvoo, Illinois, then to Adam-ondi-Ahman, Far West, Liberty Jail and Independence, Missouri. Although there was nothing to see at Adam-ondi-Ahman except a marker, it was by far our most spiritual experience among some gigantic spiritual and historical experiences. It was on a

čool, crisp fall day. I explained to both buses that they would see nothing but they would be walking where Adam walked and to use it as a time of reverence, reflecting on how fortunate we were to be here. The majority walked slowly with me up to a knoll that had been planted in wheat which was about an inch tall and green. We knelt and prayed and in the prayer,, asking in faith, that we might know of a surety if this was where Adam knelt. There were many that broke into tears because they felt the confirmation so strong. A Sister Erb, one of the sponsors, said she had put on a new pair of white slacks that morning and had gotten a wheat grass stain on one of the knees. I apologized. She said, "Oh please, don't apologize. I will forever be grateful for this experience. I plan to cut out the green stain part of my slacks and place it in my Book of Remembrance as a memento for one of the greatest spiritual experiences of my life!" To the non-believer this will all be baloney. To me it was real. In my case I didn't feel anything right away and was quite disappointed. I got back on the bus, sitting right behind the bus driver, pondering the whole experience. As the bus drove off, I found myself singing in a soft and pleasant voice (not mine!) what I later discovered to be the third verse of the hymn, "How Firm A Foundation." It is my testimony that those were the words Elohim spoke to Adam upon his removal from the Garden of Eden: "Fear not (Adam) I am with thee,

QUESTIONS REGARDING THE CHURCH OF JESUS CHRIST

oh be not dismayed for I am thy God and will still give thee aid. I'll strengthen thee, help thee, and cause thee to stand, upheld by my righteous omnipotent hand." Then the tears came and I quietly cried all the way to Far West, Missouri, a distance of about 20 miles. It is a sacred experience to me.

53. <u>Paul taught not only by word but by example that there should be an unpaid ministry. Is that the practice of your Church today?</u>

1. See ARE MORMONS TEACHING FABLES for a more complete answer as to what Paul taught.

2. Today, all Ward and Stake Leaders including Bishops and Stake Presidents support themselves although they may work more than 8 hours a day in their calling. Younger missionaries and older couple missionaries support themselves, possibly with the help of family and ward members in some cases.

3. The General Authorities, in some cases, receive an allowance (not a salary!) for living expenses which in no way reflects the service they render.. It has no bearing as to the prosperity of the Church, the amount of hours they render or how much money they bring into the Church as is the case with other churches. In most cases, the General Authorities provide for their own care.

4. It has pretty well been the same since the Restoration. People helped out Joseph Smith, Jr. while he was translating. When he wasn't he worked to provide for his family such as in 1830, working in the fields. In Nauvoo, he opened a store to provide for himself and his family. Like Paul, he was given permission to use Church resources (meager) D&C 25 but usually did not do so. Brigham Young said that all he (Brigham) ever received from the Church was a ham on one occasion. Otherwise, he also supported himself and his family.

54. What was the Council of Fifty?

1. See the Encyclopedia of Mormonism for complete details.

2. It was a theocratic form of political government that operated under the First Presidency and was organized in Nauvoo in 1844. Its goal was to see that the government operated according to scripture, not payoff, blackmail and coercion as was so prevalent then and may be still true to some extent. The Fifty helped in the presidential campaign of Joseph Smith, Jr. but his assassination stopped that. They helped in the westward migration of the Saints from Nauvoo and that is about it except for a brief period while President John Taylor faced such severe trials. The Antis try to attach some mysterious role to their existence which is just more baloney.

55. If the Three Witnesses were excommunicated for lying, etc. possibly they were lying about the plates?

1. None were excommunicated for lying, cheating, stealing or for drunkenness. (More of the Antis' hogwash)

2. Martin Harris (1783-1875)"I "...didn't ever leave the Church, the Church left me." This was in 1837. Although no evidence exists that he was never officially excommunicated, he was rebaptized on November 7, 1842. He stayed on in Kirtland and acted as self-appointed guide-caretaker of the Kirtland Temple for a number of years. He listed himself on the 1860 Kirtland census as "Mormon Preacher." Brigham Young invited him to come to Salt Lake City in 1856 and his wife, Caroline and the children did. He finally came in 1870. He loved to bear his testimony about the vision. He would, when asked if he really believed he had seen an angel, respond, "No, I don't believe it, but my disbelief is swallowed up in my knowledge that I did see an angel, that it was in the brightness of day, and the angel testified to us of the correctness of the translation." Remember, back then your word was everything to you.

3. Oliver Cowdery (1806-1850) His wife said of him after his death, "He always without one doubt...affirmed the divinity and truth of the Book of Mormon." Oliver left the Church over the polygamy issue and Joseph telling him he should live the United Order and not keep his

land out of it. He was excommunicated in 1838, none of it having to do with lying, cheating or stealing. In his ten years outside the Church, (he rejoined the Church in 1848) he never succumbed to the considerable pressure to deny his Book of Mormon testimony.

4. David Whitmer (1805-1888) The most interviewed of the Three Witnesses. He was unwavering in his testimony, although he was excommunicated in 1838 along with his brother-in-law, Oliver Cowdery. He took up residence in Richmond, Missouri, and was a very respected citizen and businessman there for fifty years. It was reported that he had denied his testimony on one occasion, shortly before his death. He took out a full page ad, having all the town's most respected men sign that David's word was his bond. He then said in the advertisement that he had never denied it and testified of the correctness of his testimony in the front of the Book of Mormon.

56. I have heard that Joseph Smith rewrote or revised parts of the Bible. If it wasn't correct the first time, why should I believe it the second?

1. The reason for the revisions was that in the translation from the different languages many plain and precious truths had been lost. For example, in the CONTRADICTIONS IN THE NEW TESTAMENT most all of them are cleared up by Joseph's revisions.

QUESTIONS REGARDING THE CHURCH OF JESUS CHRIST

57. <u>Was Satan Jesus' brother? How can someone so evil be brothers with someone so righteous?</u>

   1. Yes

   2. You don't have to go far to find the same thing. Abel and Cain are perfect examples. So are Nephi and Laman. There are plenty of examples around us today, where one brother is almost Christ-like and the other is almost Satan-like.

58. <u>Do Mormons condemn the Catholic Church for teaching the infallibility of the pope?</u>

   1. We don't condemn them but it is certainly an incorrect principle. They are human. Study the popes and you will find that they were a little too human, such as Pope Alexander VI. His terrible deeds including charging for forgiving sins, (one of the milder misdeeds) and murders by poisoning) were the reason for the Reformation started by Martin Luther in 1517.

59. <u>Has Joseph Smith ever received false revelations?</u>

   1. No, but many, including some of the leaders such as David Whitmer and Oliver Cowdery, thought so when in 1836 Joseph predicted that the Kirtland Safety Society notes will one day be as good as gold. Later, he warned the officers that they were being too speculative and he

resigned from the Society but since he had prophesied the above they thought it was okay to keep on. The bank went broke in 1838. However, in 1847 in Utah the notes were used and put on par with gold since they had no other currency!

60. <u>What about the Reorganized Church? When did it start? What are the differences in its policies?</u>

   1. They tried to start it in 1856, 12 years after Joseph had been martyred. They (Zenas H. Gurley, Jason W. Briggs and William Marks) decided to try to enlist Joseph Smith III as its president on the patriarchal order so it would draw more people. He refused. He failed at business so the next time they asked in 1860 he agreed and so the church was organized with approximately 300 people. Today membership is around 200,000 compared to our 16,000,000.

   2. They reject much of the Doctrine and Covenants including any referral to plural marriage, celestial marriage, endowment or sealing and the Word of Wisdom. Their ministers may smoke and since 1988 the women have held the priesthood. They have at times voted down "revelations" that their president has received-one year voting down 3 out of 4. They are ecumenical in their belief which means one church is as good as another. Since they are actually protestant (one who protests)

in nature they do not emphasize the Book of Mormon. In fact, to join the National Council of Churches they had to de-emphasize the Book of Mormon, the vision of Joseph Smith, Jr and its translation by the gift and power of God.

61. <u>I'm too old, why do I need to change</u>

1. Mosiah 2:36-41; Alma 5:49; Alma 34:32-34; Moroni 10:3-5; D&C 1:14-16; D&C 45:1-2. My mother joined at age 62 and my grandmother joined at age 87 years young! What a great day it was when we all went to the holy temple together to be sealed for all eternity. They both said (both are now deceased) that the years following their baptism were the happiest days of their lives.

62. <u>Was Jesus Chist created first? Where does it say it in the Bible?</u>

1. John 1:1 "In the beginning was the Word (Jesus Christ- in 14-the Word was made flesh) and the Word was with God, and the Word was God, 2. The same was in the beginning with God. 3. All things were made by him (Jesus Christ); and without him was not any thing made that was made."

2. One of Jesus' titles is the Firstborn. See Psalms 89:27; Isaiah 41:4; Colossians 1:15; Hebrews 12:23).

3. The clearest answer comes from Moses 6:26

BIBLIOGRAPHY:

Doctrinal New Testament Commentary Volumes I-II by Bruce R. McConkie.

Euscbius' Ecclesiastical History by Eusebius Pamphilus, Bishop of Caesarea in the fourth century.

In His Many Mansions By Rulon S. Howells

Doctrines of Salvation Volumes I-H by Joseph Fielding Smith

Mormon Doctrine by Bruce R. McConkie

Evidences of Book of Mormon in Ancient America by Dewey Farnsworth

Encyclopedia of Mormonism Volumes -IV

Journal of Discourse Volumes 1-26

Articles of Faith by James E. Talmadge

THE STANDARD WORKS along with the Topical Guide and Bible Dictionary

If you have read all of this, I hope and pray that you have enjoyed it. We started out by asking if the Mormons are teaching fables. After reading all of it, I think you will agree with me that the Church of Jesus Christ of Latter Day Saints is the only Church that practices what Paul taught. It doesn't mean that the others are all wrong but they do not have the complete Gospel of Jesus Christ. If you have positive feedback or questions after reading the book, please feel free to contact me at mormonfables@yahoo.com

Printed in the USA
CPSIA information can be obtained
at www.ICGtesting.com
LVHW032032310723
753579LV00003B/3/J

9 781977 261861